LOVE:
The
Atomic
Power
of Believing.

You are all that He is in you.

By D. Micheal Cotten

Love: The Atomic Power of God

ISBN# 978-1-936497-33-1

Contact the Author at
dmichaelcotten@att.net

Searchlight Press
Who are you looking for?
Publishers of thoughtful Christian books since 1994.
PO Box 554
Henderson, TX 75652-0554
info@Searchlight-Press.com
www.Searchlight-Press.com

Table of Contents

Notes

Introduction

In this book the objective is to differentiate the life offered to Believers by GOD and the life that many Christians lead because they never break away from depending on their own abilities to guide and provide for their existence. To this end, the word Believers is used to describe a Christian who believes and is trying to unplug from their own abilities and plug into the power of GOD Almighty living inside Believers. Believer is a future perfect tense meaning; to constantly be believing in Jesus Christ.

Almighty God's "Unseen forces" in the world will be investigated; Atoms, DNA, and Love. Love is the unseen source of power in the Believer's Kingdom of GOD and will be explored, to understand GOD's love for all and the Believer's love for God as a source of power. At the heart of this power is belief in GOD, and GOD's love for creation of the World and Mankind. Love is more than a feeling; it is the source of power motivating GOD to send His son to die for the sins of mankind and the motivation for Jesus Christ to sacrifice Himself for Believers.

Discovering the truth about the ownership of the world and everything in it, will begin to illuminate GOD's plan for Believers. Embracing the "Creation of All", acknowledges there is a "Creator of All" and is paramount to Believers' trust in GOD. It is Trust in GOD that pleases and opens the windows of GOD's Grace for Believers. Comprehending the old expression, "You can't take it with you." becomes paramount in evaluating what Believers choose to give value, time, and effort in our daily living.

The new life in Jesus Christ involves being born into a new family and we will explore embracing our new Father, Brother, and best friend. The Bible says all things become new and old things are passed away, this truth must be firmly planted in our hearts so that we can draw on our new life and family and not make decisions based on the pre-Christian system of thought.

How do we discover the Believer's part of GOD's plan? What is the balance between resting in GOD's provision and a Believer's responsibility to act in faith and not be slothful? Believers are "Dead to the law" so that we can be "Married to Jesus Christ." How can part of a Believer's responsibility be, to labor to stay in GOD's "Promised Land", or "GOD's Rest", or "The Kingdom of GOD"?

GOD is living inside every Believer and therefore GOD is here and now. If you believe GOD is inside you, you can have confidence that GOD hears your prayers, knows your every thought, emotion, and action. GOD is not inside you to condemn or judge Believers but to empower and lead Believers.

Words from the Author

Writing Style

This book is not written in strict adherence to grammatical rules. The Bible and concepts of God are complicated. To unpack the compound sentences of the Bible and the interaction of the seen and unseen worlds, every page will contain highlights, capital letters, quote, underlines, and cascading stanzas, to add sound to the written word.

Understanding GOD's Plan
Old Covenant - New Covenant
Before the Cross – After the Cross

The New Covenant does not start at Mathew 1:1, the new covenant does not start at Jesus birth, the New Covenant does not begin until Jesus takes the sins of the entire world and offers forgiveness to all believers. When studying the Word of GOD, Believers must rightly divide the Word of GOD. One of the keys to understanding GOD's Word is to examine which covenant the scripture references. Your red letter edition of your Bible is important but the words Jesus spoke must be rightly divided into the context that applied to Old Covenant and/or the New Covenant. The requirements for Believers' actions before the Cross and after the Cross are completely different. The difference in the context may cause Believers to fall victim to a performance based Christianity that is far below the level of Life Jesus died to give Believers.

Context of the New Testament people in the life of Jesus Christ.
> No one that received Healing had received Salvation.
> None of the Disciples had received Salvation until Acts 2.
> Jesus family was not saved until the Cross was finished.
> No one Jesus raised from the dead had received Salvation while Jesus was alive on earth.
> Many of the Lord's teachings are based on the only covenant available before His Death and Resurrection.

Instructions in context to the Old Covenant (Pre-Cross)
Listen to the words of Jesus regarding Salvation to the rich young ruler;
> And a certain ruler asked him, saying, Good Master, **what shall I do to inherit eternal life?** And Jesus said unto him, Why callest thou me good? none is good, save one, that is, God. **Thou knowest the commandments,** Do not commit adultery, Do not kill, Do not steal, Do not bear false witness, Honour thy father and thy mother. And he (the young ruler) said, All these have I kept from my youth

up. Now when Jesus heard these things, he said unto him, Yet lackest thou one thing: sell all that thou hast, and distribute unto the poor, and thou shalt have treasure in heaven: and come, follow me. Luke 18

Before the Lord's Sacrifice for Sin, "the way" to Salvation was **Do the Commandments and follow Jesus.**

Instructions in context to the New Covenant (Post-Cross)
Now listen to Paul in Acts talking to the Jailer about Salvation;

> And at midnight Paul and Silas prayed, and sang praises unto God: and the prisoners heard them. And suddenly there was a great earthquake, so that the foundations of the prison were shaken: and immediately all the doors were opened, and every one's bands were loosed. And the keeper of the prison awaking out of his sleep, and seeing the prison doors open, he drew out his sword, and would have killed himself, supposing that the prisoners had been fled. But Paul cried with a loud voice, saying, do thyself no harm: for we are all here. Then he called for a light, and sprang in, and came trembling, and fell down before Paul and Silas, and brought them out, and said, Sirs, **what must I do to be saved?** And they said, **believe on the Lord Jesus Christ, and thou shalt be saved, and thy house.** Acts 16

This miracle of Salvation was not available when Christ was teaching on Earth but available to Believers after Jesus went to the Cross.

Confirmation in context with the New Covenant (Post-Cross)
The Apostle John also confirms Belief in Jesus Christ, without any required performance, is the way to eternal life and the context is the New Covenant.

> For God so loved the world, that he gave his only begotten Son, that **whosoever believeth in him** should not perish, but have everlasting life. For God sent not his Son into the world to condemn the world; but that the world through him might be saved. John 3:16-17

Living the life Jesus describes in the Sermon on the Mount is a fruit of receiving God's Son and His love, it is not Salvation. Salvation is the "turning point" of unbelief in a GOD; to believing in GOD. The choice resulting in being a child of GOD, and being adopted into a new Family with a new Brother and Father and Friend.

Performance based teachings about forgiving to get forgiven. Change after Resurrection

Jesus tells Believers in Matthew 6 to forgive others and God will forgive us. The next three scriptures reveal a requirement or performance required before blessing from GOD.

> And forgive us our debts, as we forgive our debtors. Matthew 6:12
> For if ye forgive men their trespasses, your heavenly Father will also forgive you: Matthew 6:14
> But if ye forgive not men their trespasses, neither will your Father forgive your trespasses. Matthew 6:15

Teachings after the beginning of the New Covenant (Post Cross)

Paul tells Believers that we have been forgiven for all sins by Christ Jesus and therefore Believers should forgive others.

> And be ye kind one to another, tenderhearted, forgiving one another, even as **God for Christ's sake** hath forgiven you. Ephesians 4:32
> **Beloved, if God so loved us, we ought also to love one another. I John 4:11**

Forgiveness is no longer performance based, a Believer's forgiveness came at the Cross. Forgiveness is still important to the Human experience. Acknowledging His forgiveness toward us so that we can forgive and stay in the Lord's Peace is very important. Jesus did away with the universe of sin, now Believers can forgive hurts from others because we have been forgiven and loved by GOD. Now that I know I am forgiven of every sin; when I do something I am not proud of doing, I still apologize to Lord Jesus acknowledging His sacrifice and love for me, but not asking Jesus to come die again as if his sacrifice did not cover this new transgression.

Re-defining the word "love" from John 3:16 "For GOD so loved the world."

Mankind's culture and lifestyle are unable to process the word "Love" and give it the definition or meaning that can adequately describe love used in the Bible in John 3:16. We point to the Greek language as being the most descriptive language and that "love" in the Greek language has at least three levels of love described by three different words.

Eros	Erotic, sensual attraction
Phileo	Friendship, social, moral, direction
Agapoa	Group, family affection Root word to Breath
Agape'	Affection, GOD kind of Love

Believers and scholars, with correct intentions, have allowed these three or four words and the world view to minimize "love" to be a feeling or an expression of caring or sexual instincts. **<u>A more correct analysis of Love from GOD, is GOD's Love is the opposite of evil.</u> The actions of evil are;** revenge, greed, judgment, and more works of the flesh; revealing that there are two motivating factors in the world and **one is love** and the other is evil.

If Believers just say, "It is a God kind of love." and leave it, Believers will miss the magnitude of the omnipresence of the Holy Spirit inside us. The Apostle John uses the word "Love" in his writings more than all the other books in the New Testament and gives Believers the clearest picture of Love and GOD. Listen to the simple but profound factual description of Love and GOD in 1st John.

> He that loveth **not,**
>> knoweth **not** God;
>>> **for God is love.** 1st John 4:8

How do Believers process the fact that "GOD is Love"?
Believers must step out of our Earthly Christian culture and its norms to endeavor to understand the New Creation Life provided by the height, length, and breadth of GOD's love. **It is GOD's love that powers the world and eternal life for Believers. God's Love is the "Perfect Universe of Goodness" with GOD's corresponding actions of caring, giving, sustaining, and supplying. Believers must elevate our thinking above man-made connotation of God's love to begin to understand the motivation of GOD to create the earth, and mankind.**

If you believe a wrong principle, your life will be headed in the wrong direction. Even a small error after many years will lead you from the truth and result in a life falling short of the life Jesus came to give Believers. Any error needs to be corrected by rightly dividing the word and communication with the Holy Spirit. It is the truth **you know** that sets you free.

Chapter 1

All you need is GOD's love.

It is the Covenant of love with GOD that makes the world go round. The physical world is here to give our bodies; food to eat, water to drink and air to breathe, but our destiny and purpose is to develop a relationship with GOD Almighty, in the Spiritual world on Earth, right now. The Bible describes GOD's love for the world and mankind, and it gives Believers mental pictures to see into the Spiritual and material worlds. Listen to John, the Apostle, tell us about the totality of loving and being loved by GOD.

Beloved friends, let us love one another;
> because love is from God; and
>> Everyone who loves has God as his Father
>> and knows God.
>>> Those who do not love, do not know God;
>>> because **God is love.**
>> Here is how God showed his love among us:
>> God sent his only Son into the world,
> so that through him **we might have life.**

Here is what love is:not that we have loved God,
> but that he loved us and
>> sent his Son to be the propitiation for our sins.
>>> Beloved friends, if this is how God loved us, we
>> likewise ought to love one another. 1st John.

Note; The "life" that died in Adam and Eve is "born again" through Jesus, **inside Believers** and the "new life" looks like the image of GOD. Changes in a Believer's life don't come from praying to GOD in the Heavens but uniting with the GOD inside you to change your physical world, by appropriating the finished works of Jesus available to Believers.

To make the connection to the physical, world a Believer must speak from the motivation of the Spirit and act on the word of GOD. The power of the finished works of Christ and the fruit of a Believer's

Spirit must be released (activated) not summoned from Heaven; GOD is inside you. GOD wants to have a relationship with his creation. Do you want a relationship with GOD? A Believer must want to know GOD more than ourselves? Is GOD part of your personal destiny and purpose? If you don't cultivate a relationship with God you will not live, you will just exist and die.

The invitation to receive Salvation, the free gift of "life" from Jesus Christ, is ever-present.

> **Rom 10:9** That if thou shalt confess with thy mouth the Lord Jesus, and shalt believe in thine heart that God hath raised him from the dead, thou shalt be saved.
> **Genesis 7:1** And the LORD said unto **Noah, "Come" thou and all thy house into the ark; for thee have I seen righteous before me in this generation.**
> **Matthew 11:28** "Come" unto me, all ye that labor and are heavy laden, and I will give you rest. Take my yoke upon you, and learn of me; for I am meek   and lowly in heart:and ye shall find rest unto your souls. **For my yoke is easy, and my burden is light.**
> **Revelation 22:16** I, Jesus have sent mine angel to testify unto you these things in the churches. **I am** the root and the offspring of David, and the   bright and morning star. **And the Spirit and the bride say, "Come". And let him that heareth say, "Come". And let him that is athirst "come". And whosoever will, let him take the water of life freely.**

Think about each scripture and our loving GOD inviting us to "Come" not ordering Believers to "Go". Take the water of the "Born again Life" freely.

Love is the Active Power of a Relationship with Almighty GOD.

Believers only have **one requirement** in the Kingdom of GOD and that is to **"love GOD and receive God's love.** There is no other requirement and a "born again life" lived loving GOD will result in right living, happiness, and satisfaction.

The Apostle Paul says it this way,
Rejoice evermore. (For the creation GOD made for you)
     Pray without ceasing. (To the God that is inside you)
         In everything give thanks: (For the gifts of GOD)
           for this is the will of God
             in Christ Jesus concerning you.
               Quench not the Spirit.
            Despise not prophesying's.
        Prove all things;
      hold fast that which is good.
    Abstain from all appearance of evil
And the very God of peace sanctify you wholly
    and I pray God your whole spirit, soul, and body
       be preserved blameless unto the coming
         of our Lord Jesus Christ.
Faithful is he that calleth you, **who also will do it.** 1st Thessalonians 5:16
Notice; The Lord will give Believers power and **preserve Believers'
bodies, soul, and Spirit blameless unto the coming of the Lord. Jesus
will do it. The power of God is inside you and wants to supply your
wholeness.**

Everything you need to know
about having
a relationship with GOD.

Jesus said, that all the commandments could be summed up in "Love your
God with all your heart and your neighbor as yourself" all other actions
spoken of in the Bible are suitable for instruction but **belief in GOD,** love
for God, and receiving of God's love is the way to change the Believer's
existence on Earth to our "new life" in Christ Jesus in the Kingdom of
GOD. The Kingdom of GOD is the invisible, eternal, realm of the Spirit
inside Believers; controlling the world outside Believers.
Remember
    GOD said "Let there be light and there was light."
    GOD said, "Whosoever believeth on Jesus Christ shall have eternal

life."

Jesus told Believers to speak to this mountain, be thou removed and cast into the sea and it will obey you.

A Believer's relationship with GOD is belief based, voice activated, and faith acted. Your voice is used in prayer, praise, worship, prophesying, preaching, raising the dead, healing the sick, speaking to the mountains of life and much more.

Unbelievers do not have life in their Spirit because unbelievers don't believe in GOD. Only with belief in Jesus Christ is your Spirit alive.

Everything in the material and Spiritual world is made by GOD for you.
When you realize that GOD loves this world and everything in it,
You may be able to see yourself as GOD's beloved.

Your relationship with God is a reflection of your belief in GOD
GOD has provided His love for Believers
as Creator, Redeemer, and Father.
A Believer's actions prove belief in the New Creation life.
A Believer's knowledge of GOD's Word changes old patterns.

Out of a Believer's heart flows a new language based on GOD's love.
And a Voice activated authority inside the Believer reigns over the issues of life.

God, at Creation, created a place for Himself inside Mankind. God made the inner sanctum in Mankind for God and Man's Spirit to be together. **The Spirit of Man created or born again** is without sin and cannot sin and therefore qualifies to be united with the Holy Spirit in the inner sanctum of Believers.

Listen to the scriptures in Romans. (Romans 8:2 and 8:10).

For the "law of the Spirit of life in Christ Jesus" hath made me free from the law of sin and death". Romans 8:2

And if **Christ be in you,** the body is dead (will die) because of sin (Adam and Eve's); but the Spirit is life (Eternal) because of righteousness. Romans 8:10

We are a new Spirit creation living inside an old body
Interconnected through the mind of Christ
there is no law from which to accrue judgment for sin,
there is now therefore no condemnation,
we are now seated with Jesus in Heaven,
we are now the fruit of the work of the Lord's sacrifice
and each believer is our Lord's gift of glory to the Father.

The Believer's challenge is to access the power from a Believer's inner sanctum to affect the visible world from the Spiritual world to accomplish the will of GOD and live the abundant life. The simplest example, is to call on joy to change a negative situation. Joy is in your Eternal Spirit, it is yours.

God spoke the worlds into existence after designing them in their intricacy and interdependence. The power of Mankind to express his mental prowess and control his existence is and was with his mouth.

> A man's belly shall be satisfied with the fruit of his mouth; and with the increase of his lips shall he be filled. Death and life are in the power of the tongue: and they that love it shall eat the fruit thereof. Proverbs 18:21

The power of your mouth to produce life is in your heart and Spirit. **Your Spirit is a new creation, it is not subject to the world in the way that your body and your mind are subject.** Your Spirit is invisible and has powers, it is loaded with the fruit of the Spirit which is love, joy, peace, longsuffering, gentleness, goodness, self-control, and faith. These powers are in your Spirit, they are yours. For example: A Believer can choose joy instead of depression, longsuffering over revenge, gentleness instead of critical judgments, faith to move the mountains of life out of the way. The choices you make can be voice activated, to enhance their value to the other senses of the body. (Ears and eyes) These and more attributes of your Spirit are in you to be used by Believers for the Believer's abundant life. **God is not going to activate the power in your Spirit (for you) it will be the Believer's choice.** Happiness is your choice along with all the other promises of GOD. You don't have to pray for the Fruit of the Spirit it is yours, you own it, it is your inheritance. In addition to the Fruit of the Spirit available to your Spirit, a **Believer's** spirit can unite with the Holy Spirit and the mind of Christ and affect the physical world with the power of the Spiritual world through the Gifts of the Holy Spirit.

The problem for Believers

The evil influence to react to the world, with works of the flesh, is the battle Believers are fighting. Believers can reign with the power of GOD inside Believers by calling on a word from their Spirit to resist the influence of evil. The world is being bombarded with the words of death; Believers must know the words of life to affect the seen world with the power of the Spiritual world.

Listen to these verses from James;

> **This is not the wisdom that comes down from above,** but is earthly, unspiritual, demonic. For where (strife) jealousy and selfish ambition exist, there will be disorder and every vile practice.
>
> **But the wisdom from the beginning, (above)** is first pure, then peaceable, gentle, open to reason, full of mercy and good fruits, impartial and sincere. James 3:15-17

These scriptures embody the influence from Satan and demonic spirits that Believers encounter and have to rise above to choose Wisdom from the Holy Spirit to stand against the enemy. Remember the Holy Spirit is inside you, **the victory is yours.**

Believers have been adopted in to GOD's Family and been given The Lord's name.

In today's culture "names" are thrown around without thought to the power of words, GOD changed the name of 5 people, in the Bible, to enlarge their vision for the individuals; Abraham, Sarah, Jacob, Peter, and Paul. In the Spiritual world names are powerful and always fulfill their name. Fortunately, Believers have been adopted into God's family and given God's family name. Believers, who don't read the will or ask the Lord about the inheritance, will live without their inheritance and without their new name. The Name of Jesus **is above every name that has ever been named.** (Ephesians 1:21and 3:15, Philippians 2:9) **The "name" Jesus has**

The Atomic Power of Love, 17

given to Believers it is above the name of death or cancer or poverty.

In Addition to a Believer's New Name, the "New Creation life", is the only realm where Believers are omnipresent with Jesus through the Holy Spirit. **The Parallel inter-connected Life in Believers is "made in the image of GOD" and in covenant with GOD Almighty. There is power in a Believer's new name and in the new Eternal life inside the Believer.**

Believers must activate their inheritance to accomplish good acts the Lord has planned for us to do. The Holy Spirit and power is available from the Spiritual world inside Believers. The important word is available, you must believe in your inheritance and you must know what a Believer inherited and then act on that power.

Listen to Paul talk about the power inside Believers.

> However, **if the Messiah, Jesus, is in you,** then, on the one hand, the body is dead because of sin; **but, on the other hand, the Spirit is giving life because God considers you righteous.** And if the Spirit of the One who raised Jesus from the dead is living in you, then the One who raised the Messiah Jesus from the dead **will also give life to your mortal bodies through his Spirit living in you.** So then, brothers, we don't owe a thing to our old nature that would require us to live according to our old nature. For if you live according to your old nature, you will certainly die; but if, by the Spirit, you keep putting to death the practices of the body, you will live. All who are led by God's Spirit Are God's sons. **For you did not receive a spirit of slavery to bring you back again into fear;** on the contrary, you received the Spirit, who makes us sons and by whose power we cry out, "Abba!" (that is, "Dear Father! Or Daddy").   Romans 8:10-15

Believers must act on "**who** they are" and "**whose** they are" if you are to have an intimate relationship with GOD. It will not profit Believers that don't know what they have inherited or how to use it. Listen to Hosea from the Old Testament;

> My people are destroyed for lack of knowledge; Hosea 4:6
> From the New Testament from John;

> If ye **continue in my word,** THEN **are ye my disciples indeed;**
> ye shall know the truth, and the truth shall make you free.
> John 8:31-32

Note: It is **not** "truth" that sets you free! It is the truth you know that sets you free.

The Lord's inheritance **is access to Almighty GOD and a never ending supply of His love.** Everything Jesus left you in his inheritance is perfect in its worth. When Believers act on their inheritance they are uniting with GOD in faith and that pleases GOD and changes the seen world from the Spiritual world.

It is through the power of the invisible Spiritual world that;
> the Red Sea was parted,
>> that manna came every day in the wilderness,
>>> that the river Jordan parted
>> so that the Israelites could enter the Promised land
> and all of the miracles of the new testament.

It is through the power of the invisible Spiritual world that;
> All Believers have been saved.
>> All believers are filled with the Holy Spirit.

The best **Birthday** present ever
For the New Creation Born again experience.

Believers are the Temple of the Holy Spirit and the Holy Spirit is inside Believers to reveal the profoundest depths of GOD. Everything we learn about GOD is a gift of love to make our lives meaningful, complete, prosperous, and lovely. Listen to this description of God's gifts to Believers from Corinthians.

> But, as the Bible says, **"No eye has seen, no ear has heard and no one's heart has imagined all the things that God has prepared for those who love him."** It is to (believers) us, however, that God has revealed these things. How? Through the Spirit. For the (Holy) Spirit probes all things, even the profoundest depths of God. **For who knows the inner workings of a person**

The Atomic Power of Love, 19

except the person's own spirit inside him? So too no one knows the inner workings of God except God's Spirit. Now we have not received the spirit of the world **but the Spirit of God,** so that **we might understand the things God has so freely given us.** 1st Corinthians 2:9

When you hear and read that Believers have the Spirit of GOD inside and that the Holy Spirit will help **to understand the things GOD has given Believers. How does that make you feel?**

Have you asked the Holy Spirit,

"What does this scripture mean?" and

"What does GOD have for you

that you don't comprehend

that you could not see, or hear,

or even imagine in your mind?"

And what are we, as Believers, doing to understand the new **level of life,** GOD has for Believers? **Believers must talk, study, and listen to the Holy Spirit inside them or miss the presents and presence GOD has for Believers.**

The Holy Spirit is inside Believers to encourage you to act in faith according to the righteousness of Jesus Christ given to Believers.
John 16:5-10,

The Holy Spirit is **not here** to convict the Christians of their Sin <u>because He has already accomplished that before you became a Believer.</u> The Holy Spirit is here to convict you of "the righteousness" you received from the overpayment of your sins; past, present, and future by the grace of Jesus Christ. When you see in your Spirit, the love and sacrifice made just for you, that intimacy with GOD, The Holy Spirit, and Savior will produce right living. (That does not mean that you will act perfectly). Your culture, habits, and the devils influence will try to keep you questioning your relationship with GOD. The enemy's influences are well known; strife, greed, anger, revenge, pride, lust, et cetera **are within a Believer's ability to resist,** but it is the Believer's choice. The new Life in Jesus Christ and

Intimacy with the Holy Spirit will keep your belief in the gift of Righteousness before your Spiritual eyes so you can look for the will of GOD in all situations, but it will be the Believer's choice to act. You can sin if you "want to", or a Believer can choose to team up with the Holy Spirit and follow the will of the Lord to a preferred action.

Contemplate the PURPOSE of the gift of the Holy Spirit as you read;
Nevertheless I tell you the truth;
> It is expedient for you that I go away: for if I go **not** away,
> > the Comforter will not come unto you;
> > > but if I depart, I will send him unto you.
> > > > And when he (Holy Spirit) is come,
> > > > he will reprove or **convict the world of sin,**
> > > > > (for Unsaved people)
> > > > > > **and of righteousness,**
> > > > > > (for Believers)
> > > > > and of judgment for Satan. John 16:6

Then the Lord repeated.
The (Holy Spirit) is come to reprove or **convict the world, of sin,**
> **because they believe not on me;**
> > (The real sin is not believing on Jesus Christ)
> > <u>(Speaking to Unsaved people)</u>
> > > **Of righteousness,**
> > > because I go to my Father, and ye see me no more;
> > <u>(Speaking to Believers)</u>
> **Of judgment,** because the prince of this world is judged.
<u>(Speaking to the judgment of Satan)</u>
Jesus repeats the job of the Holy Spirit so that we can understand in detail that the **Holy Spirit is to convict unbelievers of their sin, convict Believers of the righteousness of Jesus Christ** and **to judge Satan.** The reason that the Holy Spirit does not have to convict Believers of their sin is because The Holy Spirit convicted Believers of their sin when they were unbelievers. There is no sin on the Believer's account because the Lord's Sacrifice did away with sin. **<u>Believers must see the disconnect between Sinner and Saint, the Believer's choice to choose GOD, re-oriented the Adam and Eve breaking covenant with GOD.</u>**

Listen to the verse in Romans;

> Romans 4:7 Saying, Blessed are they whose iniquities are forgiven, and whose sins are covered. **Blessed is the man to whom the Lord will not impute sin.**

Jesus died for the Sins of the entire world and has exchanged His Righteousness for the Believer's sin, for this reason the Holy Spirit reminds Believers of their righteousness and GOD's love. When Believers act outside the will of God or forget who they are in Christ Jesus, the Holy Spirit who lives in the inner sanctum of Believers will remind believers **who and whose they are.** Don't allow anyone to confuse you with the teaching of the sin conscious pattern offered by reading of 1st John 1:9 as being for forgiveness of sins of believers on a daily or weekly basis. This scripture is about salvation. Jesus died for the sins of Believers past, present, and future. *See note about 1st John 1:9 at the end of this chapter.

Jesus was our Savior 2,000 years ago.
Jesus is our High Priest, today.

Think about the construction of the New Testament: Jesus was with Mankind on Earth during the Synoptic Gospels and Acts and GOD is inside Believers after his ascension in Acts. Everything that Jesus accomplished for Believers through Salvation was done two thousand years ago and must be appropriated by your faith in the gift of the Holy Spirit inside Believers by Jesus Christ.

> **Disciple,** a person training under the discipline or teaching of another. The word disciple is used in the **Gospels 200 times and in Acts 35 times.** And not one time in Paul and Peter's writings and the book of James and 1st, 2nd, 3rd John and Revelation.

Disciple is a pre-cross picture preparing the world for the sacrifice of Jesus Christ and the giving of the Holy Spirit for the formation of the Church. After the Cross, the Apostles Paul and John teach Believers about a personal, active, intimate, relationship with Jesus Christ through the Holy Spirit. Listen to the change in personification of our relationship after the Cross in the construction of the Bible.

> **In Him** meaning with GOD inside Believers and Believers inside GOD, is used 70 times in the New Testament with 66 times after

the Synoptic Gospels concentrated in John's and Paul's writings. **In Christ** is the New covenant word for Disciples. It is used 78 times after the Gospels and **not one time** in the Gospels because Jesus had not died and been resurrected. Believers can't be in Him until Jesus had been resurrected.

Brothers after the resurrection (John 20:17) Jesus tells Mary Go tell **my brothers** I am about to ascend to my Father and your Father. At His Resurrection Believers were added to the Family of GOD. Before this scripture Jesus had never referred to the disciples and entourage as brothers.

It is very important to understand what the Bible is saying in its construction, Before the giving of the Holy Spirit to Believers Jesus was GOD on Earth restricted to one body, **Jesus came as one man** and after the resurrection sent GOD in the Holy Spirit to be inside **billions of Believers.** **Jesus is our advocate (High Priest) between GOD and man,** no longer on Earth, but now has sent the person of the Holy Spirit to reside inside Believer's bodies.

Hebrews 2:9 But we do see Jesus — who indeed was made for a little while lower than the angels — **now crowned with glory and honor because he suffered death, so that by God's grace he (Jesus) might taste death for all humanity.** For in bringing many sons to glory, it was only fitting **that God, the Creator and Preserver of everything, should bring the Initiator of their deliverance to the goal through sufferings. For both Jesus, who sets people apart for God, and the ones being set apart have a common origin — this is why he (Jesus) is not ashamed to call them brothers** when he says, "I will proclaim your name to my brothers; in the midst of the congregation I will sing your praise." Also, "I will put my trust in him, . . ." and then it goes on, "Here **I am,** along with the children God has given me." Therefore, since the children share a common physical nature as human beings, **he (Jesus) became like them and shared that same human nature; so that by his (Jesus) death he might render ineffective the one who had power over death (that is, the Adversary) and thus set free those who had been in bondage all their lives because of their fear of death.**

The Atomic Power of Love, 23

Jesus has rendered ineffective the power of the enemy and given Believers **freedom from the fear of death** through the gift of Eternal life. Believers must strive to live in this freedom, GOD has given Believers. Believers who discern the freedom of "victory over death" can devote their life to believing in the other promises of GOD Almighty and use the inheritance to doing acts of kindness and bringing GOD's will to earth. **In the Kingdom of GOD,** actions are not as important as the belief or motive from which an action was derived. **Remember** It is not the confession of sins that produces salvation but it is the **belief that Jesus Christ died for your Sin** and has re-established your right standing with GOD. **Any action** accomplished in your own strength, without being led by GOD and trusting in GOD, is not in the will of GOD. The change in the New Testament, after the synoptic Gospels, of dropping the term "Disciple" and use of the term "In Christ and In Him" highlights a **Believer's new life is inside the Believer where the Holy Spirit resides not in trying to get GOD in Heaven to come down to help you.**

Jesus had to come to Earth as a man because God had given Mankind all power over the inhabitants of earth.

Mankind has the authority given by GOD for dominance on Earth because mankind has a "Body". The Devil has **no authority** on earth except the authority mankind gives him. (Because the Devil has no body. Jesus has a body, and that gave Him authority as Mankind. He used that authority for Believers' salvation, and to send the Holy Spirit to be in our bodies.)

Mankind can authorize the devil to execute his will to destroy you.
or
Believers can authorize GOD to execute GOD's will to bless Believers through the Holy Spirit inside each Believer.

GOD gave authority over the Earth to Mankind, unique in the worlds by our human body, the only way the adversary can get something accomplished in the Earth is for a Human to give up some of their authority. Jesus by conquering death and reintroducing an Eternal Spirit in

Believers conquered death and Satan. Believers have the victory and can resist the adversary and through the power in you, the enemy must flee.

Serving others with the love of God is the essence of what GOD wanted the world to experience and it will. When an action is motivated by a word from GOD, from the Holy Spirit, prayer, or from the Bible; a Believer will be successful. For example: The Holy Spirit will help Believers lay their anger down, raise Believers above judging others, remind Believers that peace means don't let the sun go down on your wrath and an expectation that any and all promises of GOD are available. It is communication with the Holy Spirit that leads a Believer to a life resting in the power and peace offered by the Lord. Can you think of one reason you haven't developed a personal, daily, reciprocal, relationship with the Holy Spirit?

If Believers **don't** have intimacy with GOD, they will not listen for GOD's voice. When Believers have a word from GOD and faith to believe the leading of the Holy Spirit, every life situation will be handled in concurrence with the will of GOD for the Believer and the situation. **If a miracle is needed, one will be available,** the age of miracles has not gone away because the GOD of Miracles has not changed. Believers **cannot** rest in GOD's power if they have not spoken to GOD or found a word from GOD. Believers must expand our knowledge of GOD's word and our intimacy with GOD so that we can hear GOD and know that GOD is speaking to us. **You must talk to GOD to get a response from GOD.**

For example: When you are confronted by a beggar on the street; do you ask the Lord for direction to give or minister to that person? If you are like the author, my mind gives me several choices and I don't know which one is best? Even when we ask the Holy Spirit for direction, the answer is not always easy to understand, but it is after asking many times, that we can better hear and know what GOD wants us to do. Every answer from the Lord will be rooted in love. **The Believer's thought of caring, for the beggar, is the beginning of not caring just for yourself.** Satan's influence is the Spiritual War Believers are fighting to act on GOD's direction in every thought, to overcome the influence of evil. GOD does not want us to give to every beggar, but GOD wants to talk to Believers about every situation.

Let us make mankind in our Image
And give them all power over everything
on the Earth.

At the time GOD made Man in His image, mankind was eternal and we were made to look like, act like, and be like GOD. Mankind was GOD of this earth and Almighty GOD gave mankind power over everything in the air, on the ground, and under the earth. This authority is still active because GOD's words are eternal.

> Then God said, "Let us make humankind in our image, in the likeness of ourselves; and **let them rule over** the fish in the sea, the birds in the air, the animals, and over all the earth, and over every crawling creature that crawls on the earth." So God created humankind in his own image; in the image of God he created him: male and female he created them. God blessed them: God said to them, **"Be fruitful, multiply, fill the earth and subdue it.** Rule over the fish in the sea, the birds in the air and every living creature that crawls on the earth." Genesis 1:26-28

Notice: Jesus had to come to earth as a man and now has his resurrection body, the devil does not have a body and therefore this promise from God does not apply to him, Satan can only get this power from a human doing his deeds. Every Believer has been given this power, it is up to the Believers to take the authority given them. The Author has not been successful commanding the fish in the seas but I know that GOD's word is forever true, so the problem is with a believer's knowledge and belief, not God's word. **Question:** Has my authority been stolen by the enemy through vain deceit or philosophy as Paul warns? In other words, have I been taught that I don't have authority or has my denominational pattern of teaching **not** revealed this power as part of the Believer's authority?

If you are in Christ and Almighty GOD is in you.
It is not heresy to say,
Believers are the God of this world

The Atomic Power of Love, 26

If you think I have gone out of bounds with this statement, describe for yourself "who and what are you?" if you abide in God and God abides in you, who and what are you? Are you uncomfortable with this statement or conflicted because you don't allow GOD to control any part of your life and don't experience anything from the Spiritual world? **Believers must believe** to receive anything from GOD, going to Church is not believing. If a Believer does not believe GOD's promises start until death, when you get to Heaven, then you will have what you believe.

Listen to this word from Paul about unbelievers.

> In their case the **god of this world** has blinded the minds of the unbelievers, to keep them from seeing the light of the gospel of the glory of Christ, who is the image of God. II Corinthians 4:4

> Little children, you are from God and have overcome them, **for he who is in you is greater than he who is in the world.** 1st John 4:4

A Believer is more powerful than Satan, who Paul calls the god of this world, because of Christ in Believers.

From the words of Jesus;

> But they which shall be accounted worthy to obtain that world, and the resurrection from the dead, neither marry, nor are given in marriage: Neither can they die any more: for they are equal unto the angels; and **are the children of God,** being the children of the resurrection. Luke 20:35-6

If you are the children of GOD, Believers are at least **God of this world.**
If Believers believe the scripture you can re-assert your authority.

Jesus Christ lived thirty years
Without the Holy Spirit to fulfill the prophecy that
Jesus was tempted in all parts as Mankind.

The Holy Spirit descended and stayed on Jesus at the Baptism of Jesus and His ministry of miracles and inspiration started. It was no small feat to live 30 years without sin and without the Holy Spirit. **Notice,** His ministry cranked up when the Holy Spirit stayed on Him. The timing and the construction of the Bible is precise because the prophecies and promises of GOD have been planned by GOD Almighty. There are aspects of the first thirty years of the Lord's life that should give Believers insight into living a life focused on the will of Almighty GOD. **Jesus did no mighty miracles or start his ministry until He was Baptized and the Holy Spirit stayed on Him.** Jesus is called the last Adam because he came to earth without sin and lived his life making Godly choices to qualify to be our sacrifice for sin. Jesus already had the mind of Christ and allowed the "inspiration to please GOD" control His life.

> For he **hath made him** TO BE **sin** for us, who knew no sin; that we might be made the righteousness of God in him. 2nd Corinthians 5:21

GOD had to make, Jesus to be sin, **because He had never sinned,** so GOD could make Believers righteous who did not do right. Now that the Holy Spirit is inside Believers, Believers can crank up their ministry of miracles and good works? **If you believe** and develop a relationship with God.

> A Believer's sin nature has been condemned and our new Spirit is righteous and can cohabitate with GOD in a believer's body.

> The largest problem for Believers is to subdue our mind, body, and emotions because they are not brand new and must be subdued daily.

> The rehabilitation of our minds and the changing of our mental motivation will change our approach toward life and God.

> The Holy Spirit is inside Believers and resurrection power is available.

Through aspects of the Lord's early life Believers can draw correlation to our new life. <u>**Believers**</u> are no longer sinners whose nature is to sin. **Now if we sin, it is because we want to sin, we made the choice.** God has condemned the sin nature and given Believers a New Creation Spirit, we are no longer subject to a sin nature. **In addition** to benefits of the mind of Christ and a new nature, Believers have the Holy Spirit as a friend that sticketh closer than a brother. The combination of our new Spirit, the Holy Spirit, and drawing on the mind of Christ allows Believers to make choices that come from our Spiritual world to rule over the visible temptations of our earthly world. **Believers are exceptional.** The Mind of Christ (1st Corinthians 2:16), has been made available to Believers at Salvation but we must renew our mind that is full of the old ways handed down by family, culture, desires of our flesh and demonic influence so that Believers can pull GOD's word from their Spirit to confront an issue of life (temptation). Contemplate these scriptures about the Holy Spirit in the life of Jesus and in our lives;

When Jesus also had been baptized and was praying, the heavens were opened, and **the Holy Spirit descended on him in bodily form,** like a dove; and a voice came from heaven, "You are my beloved Son; with you I am well pleased." Jesus, when he began his ministry, was about thirty years of age, being the son (as was supposed) of Joseph, the son of Heli, Luke 3:23

John the Baptist said, "I myself did not know him, but he who sent me to baptize with water said to me, **'He on whom you see the Spirit descend and remain, this is he who baptizes with the Holy Spirit.'"** John 1:33

And Jesus, **full of the Holy Spirit,** returned from the Jordan and was led by the Spirit in the wilderness Luke 4:1 Satan's temptation.

And Jesus **returned in the power of the Spirit to Galilee,** and a report about him went out through all the surrounding country. And he taught in their synagogues, being glorified by all. Luke 4:11

And the scroll of the prophet Isaiah was given to him. He unrolled the scroll and found the place where it was written, **"The Spirit of the Lord is upon me,** because he has anointed me to proclaim good news to the poor. He has sent me to proclaim liberty to the captives and recovering of sight to the blind, to set at liberty those who are oppressed, to proclaim the year of the Lord's favor." Luke 4:15-19

But the hour is coming, and is now here, when the true worshipers will worship the Father in spirit and truth, for the Father is seeking such people to worship him. **God is spirit,** and those who worship him **must worship in spirit and truth."** John 4:23-24

If you then, who are evil, know how to give good gifts to your children, **how much more will the heavenly Father give the Holy Spirit to those who ask him!"** Luke 11:13

Believers have the Holy Spirit or can ask the Father to give a Believer the Holy Spirit. Jesus taught the Disciples about the Holy Spirit and the Kingdom of GOD for forty days after the resurrection. Acts 1 and 2. Believers must embrace this exceptionality of the New Creation life which includes the combination of our Spirit and the Holy Spirit of GOD to reign in life. Paul later tells us about the fruit of the Believer's Spirit and the gifts of the Holy Spirit. The fruit of a Believer's Spirit is inside you and can be drawn upon at your will; love, joy, peace, faith, self-control, longsuffering and The gifts of the Holy Spirit (miracles) can be given to Believers as the Holy Spirit wills for the good of all.

* Reference from page 22
To rightly divide this scripture, we must read the context; to whom it is written and for what purpose.

1st John 1:7 But if we walk in the light, as he is in the light, we have fellowship one with another, and the blood of Jesus Christ his Son cleanseth us from all sin. (All in this connotation means All)

Verse 7 says the blood of Jesus has cleansed us (Believers) from all sin.

1:8 If we say that we have no sin, we deceive ourselves, and the truth is not in us.

This verse does not contradict verse 7 it is aimed at nostics whose beliefs system were different.

1:9 If we confess our sins, he is faithful and just to forgive us our sins, and to cleanse us from all unrighteousness. If we say that we have not sinned, we make him a liar, and his word is not in us.

This verse is not referencing Believers because there is no sin accruing to Believers' account. This verse is the Gospel of Good News for unbelievers. This 9th verse is not for daily forgiveness of wrongdoings or it would be asking the Lord to die again every day. It is the Good news of the gospel. In Addition, the next Chapter refers to Believers "My Little Children".

Chapter 2

Child of GOD
You ought to feel special.

This entire book will not say more than is said in the next paragraph, but hopefully will broaden and make it more actionable in a Believer's life. God is inside Believers and his words are written in our hearts and minds and the Lord's finished works, gifts, and promises are available for Believers to act upon.

> "This is the covenant that I **will** make with them after those days, declares the Lord: **I will** put my laws on their hearts, and write them on their minds," then he adds, **"I will remember their sins and their lawless deeds no more."** Where there is forgiveness of these, there is no longer any offering for sin. Therefore, **brothers,** since we have <u>confidence to enter the holy places by the blood of Jesus,</u> by the new and living way that he (Jesus) opened for us through the curtain, that is, through his flesh, and since we have a great priest over the house of God, let us draw near with a true heart in full assurance of faith, **with our hearts sprinkled clean from an evil conscience** and our bodies washed with pure water. Let us hold fast the confession of our hope without wavering, **for he who promised is faithful.** Hebrews 10:16-23

Notice: GOD said "I will", "I will", "I will" and GOD is faithful to honor His promises. Believers can live in victory because God has provided right standing with GOD and the gift of the Holy Spirit to live inside Believers.

> **The Blood of Jesus** has been sprinkled in the inner sanctum of the Believer where GOD abides with the Believer's Eternal Spirit.
>
> **It is a Believer's job** to activate the Spiritual world, inside Believers, affecting the seen world with the power of the invisible world.
>
> **Brothers and sisters of Jesus,** your new family allows Believers entrance to the presence of GOD with the full assurance of Faith.
>
> **There is no condemnation** because Jesus has sprinkled His blood on your conscience.

The Atomic Power of Love, 32

GOD is faithful.

The instant there was belief in Jesus Christ and repentance from self-sufficiency, Salvation created a new life inside a Believer's body. This new life is not an add-on to your physical body, you're Spirit which was dead is now alive and the new spiritual "you" is made in the image of GOD, it is exceptional. **Your new life is an interconnected parallel life to your physical body and offers exceptionality according to your belief.** The act of believing in Jesus Christ reorients the Garden of Eden fall of Mankind. Believers choose GOD and reverse the control of their existence from managing their five senses to believing in a relationship with GOD, a change from following evil to choosing good. Now, Almighty GOD is living in the interconnected parallel inner sanctum in Believers. **STOP a minute and talk to the Holy Spirit** in you. I am serious. **Stop and speak out loud to Almighty GOD who is inside you. Wait a minute and listen with your heart to your Spirit. You will feel a warmth in your Spirit. Until you believe** that GOD through the Holy Spirit is living inside you; you cannot know the truth and freedom offered by a relationship with GOD. Experiencing GOD's solidarity with you by the Holy Spirit choosing to live inside you will change and empower the way Believers live. The freedom of life lived through Jesus Christ will produce the fruit of "living right".

GOD does **not always** speak to you **at your decision to talk to GOD** but if you are expectant and ask for direction **you will receive direction.** Unfortunately, the direction from the Holy Spirit appears to always be a decision between GOD's will and man's plan. GOD's plan will always cost a believer time, substance, or love because being a servant and giving away what GOD has given you brings reward. The reward requires belief, that God is a rewarder, in the face of giving up what you already possess; time, money, and or substance. GOD gave us the example by giving His Son, first, for our forgiveness so that we might forgive.

For example: Offering an act of kindness; or being led to stop and change a tire, or paint a house for a widow, or feeding the poor, clothing the naked, visiting those in jail, and more. These acts of kindness are in everyone's ability. GOD promises to reward you on Earth and in your account in Heaven.

Warning; The next level of finding a word from the Lord, or receiving a vision, or finding the Lords will for your life, has more unknowns and uses a Believer's faith with every step.

Listen to these verses;

> **How God anointed Jesus of Nazareth with the Holy Spirit and with power.** He went about **doing good** and healing all who were oppressed by the devil, for **God was with him.** Acts 10:38
>
> When he went ashore he saw a great crowd, and **he had compassion on them and healed their sick.** Matthew 14:14

God is with Believers and the Holy Spirit and power is inside you and the power will manifest itself when you have compassion for the hurting world. This does not mean you have to go to Africa, there is a world that needs GOD's love in your house without thinking about your neighborhood or work environment.

Heart Modification, not Behavior Modification

You may be saying, I am a believer but I don't experience a very active relationship with GOD and I don't receive much interaction from GOD when I talk to GOD. What is wrong? Unfortunately, Religion has not emphasized that GOD is wanting a 24/7 relationship with Believers substituting a Sabbath day or once a week pep talk. A Believer must totally give of him or herself to having a relationship with GOD which requires time, thought, and desire. Desiring knowledge of God is an important step in cultivating a relationship with GOD. The Bible speaks of degrees of belief, Believers must believe that GOD is and that he is a rewarder of those Believers that diligently seek GOD. In Mark 4; Jesus gives readers several parables about sowing seed into the earth and in each case: The parables indicate that our relationship with GOD and the Kingdom of GOD can progress in stages. Listen to these scriptures in Mark 4.

> The Lord says, When the word planted comes forth it happens:
>> First the seed,
>> Then the ear,
>> Then the full corn in the ear.
>
> The Lord says, When the word is planted in stony soil it is starved

and dies.

> When planted in shallow soil it dries up and is starved.
> **But when planted in Good soil;** "What was sown on rich soil is the one who hears the message and understands it; such a person will surely bear fruit, a hundred or sixty or thirty times what was sown." Matthew 13:23

GOD's word when heard, with understanding, by a Believer produces fruit; 30 fold, 60 fold, or a 100 fold. The return is measured by a Believer's understanding of GOD's word. The same levels of a Believer's life and relationship with GOD are described in Romans;

> Do not be conformed to this world: but be ye transformed by the renewing of your mind, that ye may prove **what** is **that good,** and **acceptable,** and **perfect, will of God.** Romans 12:2

Notice; the levels of transformation are progressive as a Believer renews their mind.

A Believer does not have to ask **"What does God want me to do?"** but should ask **"GOD. what do you want me to be?"** GOD's instructions are written on the hearts of Believers and his written word is available. It is the understanding of GOD's word in a Believer's heart and the interconnection of a new Eternal Spirit in Believers that must be grasped for Believers to rest in God's power and accomplish GOD's will. The commitment a Believer has for the development of your relationship with GOD will determine the growth of your "New Creation Life". It is your choice. GOD has promised to meet every move toward intimacy with God with an equal or greater move of love toward the Believer.

Until you open your mind to the Spiritual world, the concept of being "Born-again" and a relationship with God is difficult to understand. Listen to the Lord speak to Nicodemus.

When Jesus spoke to Nicodemus, his question to being born again was "Can a man re-enter his mother's womb?

> Jesus answered, Verily, verily, I say unto thee, except a man be born of water and of the Spirit, He cannot enter into the Kingdom of God. That which **is born of the flesh is flesh;** and that which is **born of the Spirit is spirit.** John 3:5

Nicodemus, a very learned Hebrew, did not understand that there is a

Spiritual dimension for fellowship with God. To further complicate understanding the "born-again" experience the Apostle Paul says,

> Therefore, if any man be in Christ, **he is a new creature:** old things are passed away; behold all things are become new. 2nd Corinthians 5:14-17

**What old things passed away as you became a Believer? and
What about you is completely new? and
What are you doing with the change?**

Self-Reliance is the "old thing "about your life that is passed away (repentance) when you change the direction of your life from self-reliance to GOD reliance. This "new life" is a completely new direction in a Believer's "new life". Knowing the GOD of Creation and accepting the Salvation from Jesus Christ settles your future and crushes anxieties of existing in the physical world with death looming as the only result. **Hallelujah, Hallelujah.** No one knows how GOD will lead Believers if we allow the Holy Spirit to direct our lives. **The power to walk on water, raise men from the dead, live the abundant life, cast out demons, heal the sick, reign in life, experience things we have not even imagined that GOD has for us, who believe. In addition,** The Holy Spirit also has gifts of the Spirit to give as He wills for the good of all. The Believer has inherited all of the finished works of Jesus Christ, The Holy Spirit is inside the Believer to lead the Believer into all truth. **If you don't believe in these promises they will not happen,** you can believe that. If you don't communicate with the Holy Spirit, the Believer cannot learn about the deep things of GOD and the gifts GOD has for Believers.

Jesus did not come to make bad men "Good", **He came to make dead men Alive".** The real sin in the world is **not believing** in Jesus Christ and the love of GOD. Adam and Eve possessed an eternal Spirit and chose the Devil's lie and died Spiritually, Unbelievers have a dead spirit and can choose GOD and Jesus Christ and have Eternal life. Without Jesus Christ there is only existing and death for mankind. Nothing in the world has life without getting life from Jesus Christ. Without Jesus your heart may be pumping blood but the part of you made in the image of GOD is dead. **I**

haven't prayed for any dead men who came to life physically, but I am not going to tear any pages out of my Bible. I have prayed for people who were dead spiritually and came to life through the power of Jesus Christ. With Jesus Christ all things are possible and the "Finished Works of Jesus" are available for Believers.

There has been a change, Friend
There has been a change.

Quit thinking that GOD is way out there in space, GOD made this world for you and gave part of Himself for your redemption and wants to have an everyday relationship from inside Believers. GOD wants to be involved in everything a Believer does, the question is will you involve GOD in your life. GOD now lives inside Believers and God lives in a Holy Temple, a Heavenly Ark of the Covenant inside Believers. The Temple inside Believers is Holy, God made it Holy. God could not wait for us to "be" Holy.

> for ye are **the temple of the living God;** as God hath said, **I will dwell in them, and walk in them;** and **I will be their God,** and **they shall be my people.** 2nd Corinthians 6:16-18

Again notice GOD's words "I will dwell", "I will walk" in them, and "I will be their GOD." The Believer only believed and GOD did the rest. Will you yield your self-sufficiency to receive GOD's fullness?

The New Creation dimension in your life is a power greater than the greatest power in all of mankind, because it is the combination of the Believer's Eternal Spirit and the Holy Spirit of GOD. The beginning of a Believer's power is Eternal life, the power over death. In addition, the Believer's new family name is greater than any name of anything named and Lord Jesus is that name. Think about this fact; **Jesus is Lord of Lords and King of Kings, Believers are the Kings and the Lords.** Believers have inherited the right to use the name of Jesus to overcome physical situations with Supernatural Spiritual power. For example: You choose whether to be sad or happy, angry or in control, good or evil. It is your choice. A Believer chooses to allow the situation to dominate or to dominate the situation with the power of the Believer's fruit of the Spirit.

A Believer can allow a demonic influence to ruin his day or even his family's day, for example: A Believer can see a well-dressed man at Church and remark, "he is not smart enough to have made all that money himself", and with that statement your children leave for Sunday school and tell their classmates that the well-dressed man is too dumb to have made his money himself, and you can see the seed of demonic influence grow because you as a Believer lusted after another man's possessions instead of praising GOD for prospering the men at your Church. The power to capture that lustful thought and bring it to the Lordship of Jesus Christ was in you but not chosen. Listen to this Psalm of David, David is **commanding** his soul to Bless the Lord with everything in him and do not forget the benefits of Salvation of the Lord!!

> Bless the LORD, O my soul: and all that is within me, bless His holy name. Bless the LORD, O my soul, and forget not all his benefits:
> **Who forgiveth** all thine iniquities; **who healeth** all thy diseases; **Who redeemeth** thy life from destruction; **who crowneth** thee with loving kindness and tender mercies; **Who satisfieth** thy mouth with good things; so that thy youth is renewed like the eagle's. Psalms 103

David is taking control of his thought life and making sure His focus is on the Lord and not on fear.

When a Believer goes for a walk Almighty God goes with you.

The power of the Spiritual presence of your new Spirit and the Holy Spirit living inside you can be drawn upon to reign in life, on earth, when acting on a word from the Lord. Everyone has a word from the Lord to Love GOD and their neighbor as themselves and more. If you start everyday by thanking GOD for being able to move your limbs, see with your eyes, and hear with your ears; then lift up a prayer for all those who can't see, hear, or move; your heart will be charged up. When you see the sun rise and smile because you know the Creator you have started reigning in life. Happiness is a choice. Joy, faith, peace and more are part of your Spirit,

The Atomic Power of Love, 38

you must choose the fruit of your Spirit over the situations of the world. Jesus said, "It is finished!" on Wednesday the 14th day of Nissan in the year, 30 A.D. At that instant, the finished promises of "The Cross" were deposited in the care of the Holy Spirit inside Believers.

> The natural person does not accept the things of the Spirit of God, for they are folly to him, and he is not able to understand them **because they are spiritually discerned.** The spiritual person (evaluates) judges all things, but is himself to be judged by no one. "For who has understood the mind of the Lord so as to instruct him?" **But we (Believers) have the mind of Christ.** 1st Corinthians 2:15-16

A Believer must come to the revelation that GOD through the Holy Spirit is with the Believer in every situation all day, every day, because GOD is inside you.

When we were born of woman, we were born sinners. This is confusing because at birth we had committed no sin. Unfortunately, the offense of Adam and Eve changed the DNA for humanity from a Spirit in right standing with GOD to Humanity **possessing a sin nature (devoid of a living Spirit). As babies we were born in the flesh but not in our Spirit.** GOD said to Adam and Eve, "If you eat of this tree you shall surely die." but their bodies were still existing after they ate, but their Spirit died and evil was revealed and Adam and Eve hid from GOD and knew they were naked. As unbelievers, Mankind serves sin (the knowledge of evil) and Mankind acts as the god of its own existence. This self-sufficiency masked the need for a Savior and GOD. When Jesus sacrificed his sinless life, GOD condemned "the sin in the Flesh", changing a part of mankind; Believers had carried since birth, and giving birth to an Eternal life in the Spirit, "Born-again" in a Believer's body.

> Romans 8:3 for **what the law could not do,** in that it was weak through the flesh, God sending His own Son in the likeness of sinful flesh, and **for sin, condemned sin in the flesh:**

Notice; when believers are born again, our Spirit has come alive; we are alive in two realms, an inner sanctum, and our physical body. These two realms are complimentary, a Believer and the Holy Spirit can affect the seen world with the power of the unseen or Spiritual world. Faith to move the mountains of life; joy for mourning, self-control to alter anger, peace to snuff out fear, and more. When GOD is for you who can be against you. But you must believe that GOD "is" for you.

A Believer's new Spirit has never sinned and will never sin because the Spiritual "you" has been "made" righteous.
Listen to Paul in Romans,

> For as by one man's disobedience
> <u>**many were "made" sinners,**</u> so
> by the <u>**obedience of one (Jesus) shall**</u>
> <u>**many be "made" righteous.**</u>
> <u>**Romans 5:19**</u>

Notice the wording, <u>we were **"made"** sinners and we were **"made"** righteous.</u> Neither act was in Mankind's control. **When God makes something righteous, it is righteous.**

The Bible describes everything as a choice between sin and righteousness, but in terms for today; the question is; "are you going to choose to be motivated by the GOD of Creation, Salvation, and Sanctification or are you going to depend on yourself?" That is the choice.

Listen and think about the story Jesus used to teach the Pharisees about repentance and GOD's rest.

> "What man of you, having a hundred sheep, if he has lost one of them, does not leave the ninety-nine in the open country, and go after the one that is lost, until he finds it? And when he has found it, he lays it on his shoulders, rejoicing. And when he comes home, he calls together his friends and his neighbors, saying to them, 'Rejoice with me, for I have found my sheep that was lost.' Just so, I tell you, **there will be more joy in heaven over one sinner who repents** than over ninety-nine righteous persons who need no repentance. Luke 15:4-7

The sheep did not want to be lost and yielded (repented) to the Good Shepherd to pick it up, carry it, protect it, bring it peace and celebrate with the whole family. Jesus is our Good Shepherd.

Do not miss this!
Repentance means to change the directional force in your life. The Greek word Metanoya means "change your mind". The Church teaches that we must repent to be saved so that we can try to live Holy but scripture says,

> For by grace are ye saved through faith; and that not of yourselves: **it is the gift of God:** Ephesians 2:8

Living right is a fruit of Repentance not repentance itself. If GOD is your directional force, then "right living" is the fruit of the direction a Believer has chosen. Another description of the word; "Repent" means **to change your mind, will, and emotions** and control of your body, because of **who you are** and live unto righteousness because of the belief in **whose you are** and who is living inside you. Right living is accomplished by an act of faith in **right believing** not motivated by fear of judgment.

> I will receive you, And will be a **Father unto you,** and ye shall be my sons and daughters, saith the Lord Almighty. II Corinthians 6:18

GOD did not install in Believers a defective New Spirit, full of sin and lawlessness and agree to be inside you with your Spirit. It is Mankind's choice to believe and receive "right standing with GOD" through Jesus Christ. A Believer's born again Spirit is "made" Righteous and **Holy** by its Creator. Anyone questioning their position in Christ can make the choice to believe. It is never too late to evaluate your belief, and anyone who thinks they are a Believer and nothing has changed in their lives and they do not love GOD in their heart, **should reach out to the Lord again.** The enemy is trying to blind the minds of people hearing the Gospel.
The Apostle Paul says, **Beware!**

> In whom the god of this world hath blinded the minds of them which **believe not,** lest the light of the glorious gospel of Christ, who is the image of God, should shine unto them. II Corinthians 4:4

Have you been told that you need more faith, or to cast out a devil, or to be sprinkled, or Baptized in the Name of Jesus, or to live Holy, or fast twice a week, or tithe and give offerings, or worship on the Sabbath, bind and loose problems, put on the full armor of GOD, and many more things to do?

All of these actions or requirements are in the Bible and spoken of in today's denominations and churches but they will not bring right standing with GOD. **The Bible speaks about most of these items and there is a place for them, but the key to relationship with God is to Love GOD and receive God's love to you.**

Repent means to **change your mind, reverse your direction, or turn away from the old gods in your life,** the Church wants the definition of repent to mean; quit committing sins, and reverse your sinful ways. The only sin that matters is **not believing** in GOD and Jesus Christ's redemption for your sin. The Gospel is a free gift **not to be measured by performance** or it is not a gift. Changing your behavior is a fruit of Repentance, it is not repentance. Think of it as "Heart modification not Behavior modification". Salvation is more than a ticket to Heaven and it cannot be earned by refusing to drink, lie, or sleep around, etc. The word for Salvation in the Old Testament is "Total Wellbeing". The Greek word for Saved is Sozo or Sodzoe and is used 110 times in the New Testament and the 53 of times it means salvation the other times it is translated **to be whole, healed, delivered, to be safe,** and more.

GOD's plan for Salvation is a mystery to the world.
The very idea of dedicating your life as a Believer to a GOD you can't see, feel, or touch is a mystery to the world. The problem for unbelievers is their future is death. **Unbelievers** exist only in their own senses and trust in their own ability. Unbelievers are the god of their life serving themselves completely under the influence of the enemy.
Listen to the Apostle Paul in Corinthians,

> But God hath chosen the foolish things of the world to confound the wise; and God hath chosen the weak things of the world to confound the things which are mighty; And base things of the world, and things which are despised, hath God chosen, yea, **and things which are not (visible), to bring to naught things that are (visible)**: That no flesh (visible) should glory in his (Spiritual) presence. 1st Corinthians 1:27

Important note; Examine the last verse "that the visible world is brought to nothing by the invisible world of the Spirit inside

Believers". **The very beginning of understanding the invisible world can be exemplified by capturing our thoughts and actions. Notice the mental challenge,** even a Believer's mind, will, and emotions may lead Believers into a lawlessness situation but a Believer can choose to resist **the influence to act in the flesh** and can ask for guidance from the Holy Spirit and redirect the Believer's mind, will, and emotions. **For example:** Re-acting in anger to a bad driver is the incorrect response, but the Believer recognizing an improper thought and stopping it and bringing it to the Lordship of Jesus Christ is the correct response. Resisting the influence to anger will eliminate; strife, a spike in blood pressure, and a rush of adrenalin, allowing Believers to reign over situations in peace. Think about the decision of the young man at **the feeding of the five thousand,** the question; do you give away your lunch and chance going hungry? or do you want to be the boy who gave Jesus what he had (5 loaves and 2 fish) and watched one of the greatest miracles of all time? Follow the leading of the Holy Spirit and you will not operate out of fear of doing without lunch and you will give what you have to the Lord to see what GOD will make of it?

Be comforted,
Your Salvation does not depend on you
Your belief depends on you.

GOD did not make his new covenant with Believers, GOD made his covenant with Jesus Christ for Believers and therefore God knows that the sacrifice for sin and the execution of GOD's justice has been completed, perfectly. Do not look at your frailty, thinking you have to live up to a Godly standard of conduct but hear the scripture, **Believers must believe;** Jesus lived up to the perfect standard of conduct and has given His grace to Believers. The freedom from the judgment of sin **does not make life easy or wrong doings OK.**

The question is,

"Do you believe in God's Salvation and all of Salvation's benefits?" or

"Do you believe Salvation Benefits start when you get to Heaven?" You will receive what you believe. Your entire life is a product of what you believe. If you believe GOD, the Holy Spirit is inside you with your new Creation Spirit and has power to reign in life as the scripture states and this life is available right now. If you believe you have to suffer through this life as on old sinner saved by grace with a ticket to Heaven, then you will have what you believe.

For if, because of one man's trespass, death reigned through that one man, much more will **those who receive the abundance of grace and the free gift of righteousness reign in life through the one man Jesus Christ.** Therefore, as one trespass led to condemnation for all men, so one act of righteousness leads to justification and life for all men. For as by the one man's disobedience the many were made sinners, so by the one man's obedience the many will be made righteous. Romans 5:17-19

Redemption is a Garden of Eden experience in reverse.

Believers have difficulty embracing God's "love" because of a lack of understanding of GOD's plan. GOD's plan does not include Believer's being able to live Holy; Redemption is a Garden of Eden experience in reverse. God said to Adam and Eve, "If you eat of this tree you shall surely die" and now GOD says to the dying world.

"For GOD so loved the world that He gave his only son that **whosoever Believeth** on Him shall not perish but have everlasting life." John 3:16

Adam and Eve believed Lucifer's lie, and their belief in the lie "made" their descendants deal with a dead Spirit and a sin nature. **Believers believe** and Jesus creates in them a New Spirit and God comes to abide in Believers. Believers are blessed to be Joint Heirs to the Lord's finished works (Isaiah 53). When you were born, it was an act of mankind, when you were born-again; **it was an act of GOD, a miracle.** Consider the magnitude of God's plan. **Mankind was not able to Covenant with GOD, only Jesus is qualified to Covenant with GOD for the sin of mankind.**

Only the GOD, that created all things,

The Atomic Power of Love, 44

would sacrifice part of Himself to
supply the demands of a broken covenant and
offer eternal life to believers,
who choose right standing with GOD.
Our new Spirit Life is suspended in God's Grace, inside our inner sanctum, separated like the Ark of the Covenant in the Holy of Holies. This Temple, not made with hands, inside Believers, is shared by the Believer's Spirit and the Holy Spirit. Believers must act and speak to use the Spiritual world to control a Believer's physical world. Voice activated sharing of a Believer's life with the Holy Spirit engaged in doing acts of goodness is the way to perfecting your joy and bringing Glory to Jesus.

Wait a minute, Wait a minute.

I still do things I am not proud of doing. That is right, your Spirit has been made righteous and eternal, but a Believer's mind, will, and emotions have not been redeemed, yet. How can this be, don't we need to try to be Holy? **The answer is yes, but not as a work of the flesh.** There is absolutely no Spiritual value in the best deed possible, if done as a work of the flesh or to receive a reward. **A work of the flesh cannot please GOD. Without faith you cannot please GOD (Hebrews 11:6). All of the works of the flesh have consequences and you will suffer for not choosing right living.**

For **example:** If you eat or drink beyond moderation, the consequence is you will get fat. If you have sex outside marriage, there may be a consequence from the betrayal of your spouse or from a child being born from the affair. For the Believer, the sin will not be added to the Believer's account but the resulting consequences will create a distraction and that will change your focus from GOD and eventually causes a hardened heart.

Separating ourselves to God from an overflowing heart of love with actions of service and praise will keep Believers in the will of GOD and make the world a better place.
It is not the obedience of Believers,
that made all Believers righteous.
IT WAS THE OBEDIENCE OF JESUS CHRIST.

The Atomic Power of Love, 45

The intent of a Believer must be **to Love GOD**
And receive GOD's love to Believers
And go about doing good works,
A Believer has to release the power and authority of the finished works of Jesus Christ to have them manifest. A Believer must choose joy, happiness, and thanksgiving, and call them from your Spirit. They are yours. They have been paid in full.

My experience says that trying to Love GOD with all your Heart and to "live right" is a constant battle but I have learned to interact with my friend, the Holy Spirit, for help and support and so the fight for my thought life is two against one in my favor. At Church I received God as my Savior because I knew I was a sinner and I did not want to go to hell, then I tried to "live Holy" to avoid being punished for lusts of the flesh, but I was a constant failure and therefore lived in constant sin consciousness, condemned by my inability to control my mind, actions, and desires, **but this was not God's plan.** After discovering a balance between grace and faith, I now know that the Grace was a gift and I cannot earn it. I learned that I have an interconnected parallel life inside me that is the Temple of God and that the Holy Spirit lives inside the Temple with my "New Creation Spirit". Fortunately, GOD is not depending on my ability to live Holy, but on **my choice to believe** in Jesus and receive right standing. Remember, because of one man's disobedience **you were "made a sinner" and by the actions of Jesus Christ you were "made righteous".** Now it is the Believer's faith in GOD that will give us motivation for our actions. Remember Jesus said "It is Finished" announcing that the Lord's act of love is complete. **Believers must quit talking to GOD about all their problems and start talking to their situations about GOD.** Jesus said in Mark 11:23,

> "For verily I say unto you, that whosoever shall say unto this mountain, Be thou removed, and be thou cast into the sea; and shall not doubt in his heart, but shall believe that those things which he saith shall come to pass; he shall have whatsoever he saith.

Our inheritance, is the finished works of Jesus, and the promises of GOD. Faith in GOD's will and GOD's love is the power to change the

seen world from the Believer's connection to the unseen world. Listen to some things we received from Jesus in these scriptures;

> In fact, it was our diseases **he bore,** our pains from **which he suffered;** yet we regarded him as punished, stricken and afflicted by God. But he was **wounded** because of our crimes, **crushed** because of our sins; the disciplining that **makes us whole** fell on him, and by his **bruises** (or in fellowship with Him) **we are healed.** Isaiah 53:4-6
>
> But of him are ye in Christ Jesus, **who of God is made unto us wisdom, and righteousness,and sanctification, and redemption:** That, according as it is written, He that glorieth, let him glory in the Lord. 1st Corinthians 1:27-31

Glory in the knowledge that Jesus Christ is the very image of GOD Almighty. The Finished works include the Believer's wisdom, righteousness, sanctification, redemption, wholeness, healing and more.

Wait a minute, wait a minute.
How can love be the power that moves the world?

1st John announces that God is love. How can this be? What does this mean? Could it be that **GOD is the perfectness of all goodness and the opposite of all evil?** It is the actions motivated by evil that have caused the curse, sins of the flesh and the following of self-interest. The description of true love is laying down your life for another, like Jesus has done for mankind. Love is the ONLY motivation that will move someone to do something for another person without receiving something in return. Love is the power of the Spiritual world and controls the physical world for Believers. You may think I am crazy; Guns are more powerful than Love, no, the power of love can cause the hate in a man with a gun to put down the gun and take up the Gospel of Jesus.

Without GOD, Mankind has no reason, culture, or structure to evolve into anything more than a mammal trying to feed and clothe itself without regard for life or property. Without The God of Creation as a part of social structure, observe the treatment of women in the Middle East where men consider themselves better because they are stronger and women are considered chattel. Belief in GOD brings structure and freedom in life, in contrast, to performance based existence of the strongest and meanest. which leads to slavery.

"For GOD **so loved the world** He gave his only begotten Son."

Remember GOD gave his love first. The word for world used here is for the entire world and all its adornments, GOD loves all His creations. **When we believe and receive new life through Jesus Christ; we must become enlightened, with being "new creations" and being made in the image of GOD?** It is GOD's love that is the power to create a new life in a Believer's Spirit, Believers must believe this or you will doubt your salvation. This is personal, God loves you.

Who is this GOD that would design Mankind in His Image and create this world for Mankind and Mankind for GOD? How can the only commandment be to Love God with all our heart, mind, and soul and our neighbors as ourselves? Can the power of love be that powerful? In the past, I remember seeing bumper stickers that said, "Can you visualize World Peace?" my thought now is "Can you visualize GOD's love for the World". World Peace will only happen when GOD's love for Mankind is realized and mankind loves each other.
Remember,
       "Thy will be done on Earth as it is in Heaven".
Lucifer was expelled from Heaven for not following God's will. Our New Spirit is filled with the **seeds of the Fruit of GOD's will;** love, joy, peace, longsuffering, gentleness, goodness, faith, meekness, temperance. **There is power in our Spirit to control our mind, will, and emotions but we must activate or release it, GOD is not going to use a Believer's Faith for the Believer.** The Fruit of the Spirit that is resident in the New Creation Spirit can be drawn upon, it is ours. Believers must decide to use the fruit of the Spirit.

> ...the fruit of the Spirit is love, joy, peace, longsuffering, gentleness, goodness, faith, meekness, temperance: against such there is no law. And they that are Christ's have crucified the flesh with the affections and lusts. **If we live in the Spirit, let us also**

The Atomic Power of Love, 48

walk in the Spirit. Galatians 5:22-25

In addition to the fruit of the Believer's Spirit; The Holy Spirit inside Believers also has gifts of the Spirit (miracles) that the Holy Spirit gives as GOD wills for the good of all.

GOD's desire to have a relationship with Mankind Required a plan for Mankind's redemption.

GOD desires to have a relationship with his creation, but the relationship must be chosen by the Believers of their own volition. Six thousand plus years ago Adam chose the Devil's lie and broke covenant with GOD; Two thousand years ago Jesus gave believers the opportunity to choose the knowledge of GOOD by empowering Believers to use His Grace and Faith to be heirs to the Promise of GOD through Salvation. Believers must make the connection with the Holy Spirit to develop the relationship offered by GOD to reality. Listen to the words in Galatians 2:20.

I am crucified with Christ:
> nevertheless I live;
>> yet not I,
>>> but Christ liveth in me: and
>>>> the life which I now live in the flesh
>>> I live by the "faith of the Son of God",
>> who loved me, and
> gave himself for me.

Notice; the new life Believers live, in the flesh, is in concert with Jesus Christ in the Spirit. The Lord offers **His faith,** power, and peace not "your" faith that seems to waiver, but the unshakeable" faith of Jesus Christ" is available for Believers to act in GOD's will.

The life Believers now live, in the flesh, must be in awe of the love indicated by the voluntary crucifixion of our Lord. Each Believer will understand their value to GOD, when they realize that Jesus paid the ultimate price for each Believer's redemption. The Faith **that Jesus used** when He came to earth and suffered and died **"That Faith"** that Almighty GOD, our Father, would resurrect Him from the tomb and restore him to his position in Heaven is available to Believers. Think about laying down your life and depending on your faith in anyone, that you would be resurrected. **The Lord's Faith** is only available to Believers who can immerse themselves in understanding the Lords sacrifice and the motivation of love for Mankind. **The love and New Creation Authority is inside you in the Temple of GOD available through the uniting of the Holy Spirit and your Spirit. Generally the Believer's direction from the Spirit must be spoken and actioned by Believers to affect the physical world.** Listen to the connection Paul makes with the power within us.

> That according to the riches of his glory he may grant you to be strengthened with power **through his Spirit in your inner being,** so that Christ may **dwell in your hearts through faith**—that you, **being rooted and grounded in love,** may have strength to comprehend with all the saints what is the breadth and length and height and depth, and to know the love of Christ that surpasses knowledge, that you may be **filled with all the fullness of God.** Now to him who is able to do far more abundantly than all that we ask or think, **according to the power at work within us,** to him be glory in the church and in Christ Jesus throughout all generations, forever and ever. Ephesians 3:16-21

We have been created out of love, the most powerful force in the world, because GOD is "perfect love". Creating Mankind was an act of love and because Father GOD considers Believers family, that seed of love in creation, is inside Believers. Believers are more than our physical senses, our connection with God is inside Believers, it is a parallel interconnected spiritual life. Believers must believe in their authority to activate the fruit of our Spirit. Listen to Paul's letter to the Ephesians about GOD's love for Mankind.

But God is so rich in mercy and loves us with such intense love that,
Even when we were dead because of our acts of disobedience,
> He brought us to life along with Jesus, the Messiah —
>> It is by grace that you have been delivered. **That is,**
>>> **God raised us up with Jesus, the Messiah,**
>>> **And seated us with him in heaven,**
>> in order to exhibit in the ages to come
>> How infinitely rich is his grace,

The Atomic Power of Love, 50

How great is His kindness toward us
Who are united with Jesus, the Messiah,
For you have been delivered by grace
Through TRUSTING and even this
Is not your accomplishment, but God's gift.
You were **not delivered** by your own actions;
Therefore no one should boast.
For we are of God's making,
Created in union with Jesus, the Messiah,
For a life of good actions
Already prepared by God for us to do.
Ephesians 2:1-8

The statements above in Ephesians, Galatians, John, and Romans confirm the Life of GOD Almighty is inside Believers. The Believer's authority is **not based** on performance but on a Believer's relationship with the Holy Spirit and the Believer's Eternal Spirit. **When compassion for others, captivates the heart of Believers, the authority and power of GOD's love will be present to deliver victory over the situation that caused the compassion through the actions of a Believer's body.**
Thought provoking questions and ideas;
Where is this new realm of living?
Where there is no death, or sin,
And this new life is Eternal?
How can it be that before our conversion?
We were our own god and after,
Instantly we are a new creation.
We realize; we are the children of GOD,
The Creator of Heaven and Earth is our Father
How do we renew our mind to open up our new Spirit and
How do these worlds intersect and what are we to do?
Believers must communicate with GOD, love GOD, and receive GOD's love.

Ending thought

The Atomic Power of Love, 51

Some Denominations say the days of miracles are over,
But, there was never a day of Miracles
There is only a GOD of Miracles.
Now the GOD of Miracles lives inside you.
The greatest miracle of all is Salvation
Spiritual death to Spiritual life.
This miracle is available for Believers to give away
Other miracles are available to you, if you believe.
Believers are GOD's miracle workers on earth.
All of the Lord's Finished works are the Believer's inheritance.
We inherited Authority over all the ability of Satan.
Your miraculous spiritual life started at Belief in Jesus.
Heaven is a different time and experience, altogether.

Chapter 3

Satan is the Identity thief
Believers have become satisfied
with a powerless Religion.

Satan will rob you of "what you have" if you don't know "who you are"? If the enemy can keep you from a relationship with GOD and understanding the inventory of finished works and promises Jesus has given Believers, you will live without the victory. If a Believer does not expand the knowledge of God's Word, Satan can blind the Believer as to your identity in Jesus Christ. **Listen to these scriptures about a Believer's authority over the enemy.**

> Remember, **I have given you (Believers) authority;** so you can trample down snakes and scorpions, indeed, **all the Enemy's forces;** and you will remain completely unharmed. Nevertheless, don't be glad that the spirits submit to you; be glad that your names have been recorded in heaven." Luke 10:19-20
>
> **Throw all your anxieties upon (GOD) him,** because (GOD)he cares about you. Stay sober, stay alert! **Your enemy, the Adversary, stalks about like a roaring lion** looking for someone to devour. 1st Peter 5:7-8
>
> The thief comes only in order to steal, kill and destroy; I have come so that they (Believers) **may have life, life in its fullest measure.** John 10:10

Paul in Ephesians describes the fight for our identity as a spiritual battle not a fight against people, but against the devils influence on people and situations.

> Use all the armor and weaponry that God provides, so that you will be able to stand against the <u>deceptive tactics of the Adversary</u>. **For we are not struggling against human beings,** but against the rulers, authorities and cosmic powers governing this darkness, against the spiritual forces of evil in the heavenly realm. Ephesians 6:11-12

Understanding the Believer's authority over the enemy and our victory over the enemy with our testimony of transformation through Jesus Christ is the beginning. To further elaborate about a Believes authority, the authority is available to use our faith to follow **GOD's leading** or to be influenced by the negative spirits to cause situations and tribulations. The negative spirits of the enemy and the lust for the pleasures of the flesh are influences that allow the enemy to use the Believer's GOD given Authority.

Jesus gave Believers keys to counter the negative influences of the devil.

> But I say unto you, **Love your enemies, bless them that curse you, do good to them that hate you, and pray for them which despitefully use you, and persecute you;** That ye may be the children of your Father which is in heaven: Matthew 5:44-45

These principles from Jesus stifle the negative spirits, by using the Spiritual fruit from your salvation to stomp on the enemy's attempts to motivate a Believer to step out of redeemed character into anger, revenge, greed, and hate. Every reaction to an influence from Satan to anger, greed, revenge, et cetera sets up strongholds in your mind that cause strife.

Strife is the spirit of the enemy.
Strife ruins businesses, marriages, and homes.

Strife steals, kills, and destroys. Think about this verse in James;
Who among you is wise and understanding?

> Let him demonstrate it by his good way of life,
> by actions done in the humility that grows out of wisdom.
> **But if you harbor in your hearts**
> **bitter jealousy and selfish ambition,**
> **don't boast and attack the truth with lies!**

This wisdom (strife) is not the kind that comes down from above;
on the contrary, it is worldly, unspiritual, demonic.

> <u>For where there are jealousy and selfish ambition,</u>
> <u>there will be disharmony and every foul practice.</u>
> But the wisdom from above is,
> first of all, pure,
> then peaceful, kind, open to reason,
> full of mercy and good fruits,
> without partiality and without hypocrisy. James 3:13-17

This scripture reveals the plan of the enemy, strife has ruined marriages, homes, relationships, and businesses by the millions. Worldly wisdom is going in the wrong direction and is unspiritual and demonic. This fight is lost by many believers who don't know who they are and what they have in Christ Jesus but Believers that are ASKING, SEEKING , AND KNOCKING WILL RECEIVE, FIND, AND IT SHALL BE OPENED UNTO THEM.

If you go with GOD
you must be going the same direction.

Believers must be in a constant vigilant fight against the spirits of pride, lusts, and ambition. The problem believers fight in our culture, is our way of life, is against humility, love, and service. Dependence on oneself breeds a myopic view of the world, incased in solving the personal problems of the day. Solving problems for yourself keeps you under the control of the spirits of pride, lusts, and ambition and produce a life filled with strife. Think about it, if you have some success over the problems of life, it is your success, which leads to pride. From the time you are responsible for yourself or someone else, you have expectations of your abilities to produce works of provision, comfort, and companionship. You grow up as the "Head of the Household", "Last in Line", "CEO", "Tribal Chief" etc. unfortunately, **dependence on yourself is the main barrier** to believing in the invisible aspects of GOD and the power of the unseen Spiritual life. Believers must have an image of the love of GOD, or we cannot believe in His "Rest" (All Sufficiency). We are GOD's beloved. Keeping the image of GOD's love for Believers front and center in our focus, is the start of using the invisible forces of the Spiritual world to control the seen parts of the Believer's world.

> Proverbs 4:20 my son, attend to my words; incline thine ear unto my sayings. Let them not depart from thine eyes; keep them in the midst of thine heart. For they are life unto those that find them, and health to all their flesh. Keep thy heart with all diligence; for out of it are the issues of life.

It is **not** the responsibility of the Churches in 3 hours a week to get Believers ready for a 24 hour world and an eternal life with GOD. Churches and Denominations spend most of their time on Salvation of unbelievers. After Salvation, if Believers relegate our spiritual life to one day a week and rely on our own ability to provide our needs without ever believing and saying, "Give me this day my daily bread (total wellbeing) and depend on GOD for our provision we don't understand Salvation. **A new Believer is not always given the information necessary to understand that "Salvation" changed the Believer from having "no god" to having an Eternal GOD and new Eternal life inside them.** You cannot love GOD and receive GOD's love one day a week. If a Believer lives, even one day a week, without GOD at the center of their life they miss the love of a Father, Brother, and Friend and the power and gifts available from Almighty GOD. **In addition,** a day spent without God at the center of your life means that you are your own god for that day. Heaven forbid- humor.

You cannot have a relationship with GOD If you do not talk to HIM.

Let us investigate the difference in our conversations with GOD and the beginning conversations of Adam and Eve. GOD visited Adam and Eve in the Garden in the cool of the evening. What did they talk about?
Adam and Eve might have asked about;
"GOD, Why did you chose green for grass and blue for sky?" or
"What is the purpose of animals?" or
"What is GOD's favorite fruit?" or
"Why are men and women different?" or
What language are we speaking?
"Why are we here?"
What are you talking to GOD about? GOD is inside you and hears every word you speak. Oh and by the way, don't forget, GOD is with you for all your deeds also.

A Believer's conversation with God is with; our new Father, Brother, and Friend, a Believer's identity is secure when talking, giving thanks, and praising God. What questions and ideas would you like to talk to GOD about. GOD is inside you and always available to listen. A Believer needs to start talking to your new Father so that you can start listening and understanding the Lord's voice. The leading of the Spirit will give answers to your questions or comment on your ideas. A Believer will experience a welling up of confidence, in your Spirit, when communicating with the Holy Spirit and listening for answers. When a Believer first starts listening and receiving feedback from the Holy Spirit **beware of any leading that is not motivated from a heart of love.** There **will not be** any leading from GOD to steal, kill, or destroy.

> If God is for us, who can be against us? He who did not spare even his own Son, but gave him up on behalf of us all — is it possible that, having given us his Son, **he would not give us everything else too?** Romans 8:31-32

This is a **"Game Changer".** Can you receive **the revelation** of what GOD has for you. If GOD did not spare his Son what would He withhold from you if you ask? But, GOD is not going to come to earth again to help you with a problem, Jesus said "it is finished" and sent the Holy Spirit to be inside you. The Believer must act in concert with the Holy Spirit leading or a word from the Bible.

The Believer must know
> what is the Believer's authority
> > to activate by faith
> > > the gifts of GOD and
> > > > the finished works of Jesus Christ
> > > that are the Believer's inheritance.
> > Believers must speak the promises of GOD to
> move the gifts from the Spiritual world to the physical world.

Think about your prayer; "why ask God for what you think your needs are?" Why not ask God to provide you with what GOD wants you to receive? Believers need to take the limits off their expectations and ask God to bless them with what their heavenly Father wants for them. Every scripture of provision in the Bible points toward a "one day at a time "exercise" and highlights the importance for Believers to speak to GOD daily and to speak GOD's promises to your situations.

Prayer and praise is how Believers practice the presence of GOD.

Practice the presence of GOD by talking to GOD, it is a "Game changer" it takes faith to Believe that Almighty GOD is inside you. **Talking to GOD is evidence of your faith and belief and is the way to please GOD and confirm GOD's address inside your inner sanctum.** Having a conversation about your direction will change the way you look at every situation. If you pause at a dilemma and ask for the leading of the Holy Spirit, the leading will come to your mind. At that point, there will be a choice; to go ahead with a manmade plan and/or possible influence of the enemy or **to follow the leading of the Spirit of God.**

> For example, if you have asked the Lord to help you manage your health and weight, you will be confronted with the leading to resist eating from the Holy Spirit and dilemma of your flesh wanting the pleasure of eating. The choice will be yours.

> Example 2; Some daily actions are a choice from the first impulse to do them; Anger or love, caddy or complimentary, truth or lie, share or hoard, et cetera. The choice is yours.

One direction is going with God and the other direction is disharmony. What choice are Believers making when situations arise, the Spirit will be urging Believers to respond inside God's will and for your spiritual benefit, listen to your Spirit and see if you are not happier with your direction? GOD wants fellowship with you and to guide your paths and supply your daily needs. The enemy wants to influence a Believer's thought to question GOD's ability and create fear. GOD made the Worlds but is interested in your every step, word, and thought. Choose to do right because you love GOD.

As you draw closer to GOD, a Believer may discern a calling or a word from GOD that is encompassing your life.

> For example: You may become overwhelmed with sharing your testimony and the Gospel to the unbelievers. If you receive a calling from the Lord, GOD will meet you with boldness, and inspired words, thoughts, and miracles to accomplish the calling.

The enemy will be trying to steal your identity as a soul winner and bombarding you with thoughts of inadequacy in your ability to minister salvation, but resist the fear and stay in GOD's love and you will see the miracles of bringing the spiritually dead to Eternal life through the resurrection power inside you. It is inspiring to share the love GOD has given Believers.

Are you the god of your life and how is that going for you?

GOD's words are life and health and the basis for the answer to all of life's situations but these words must be mixed with faith from a Believer's Spirit. Question; How can GOD abide with me and I abide with GOD, when I am on Earth? How can Believers understand this new paradigm, when we can **neither see, touch, feel, taste, nor hear GOD?** Everything in our being believes in a self-controlled daily life, God did not make breakfast this morning, or get the children ready for school, it was me. Breaking the "do it yourself" reliance is a choice Believers must make, in their mind, to allow their relationship with GOD to grow. To help this transition; it helps to enumerate what Believers have accomplished and what the Creator God has accomplished. To get this started;

> Believers **haven't made anything** that did not use something God created, and
> On GOD's side of the ledger of things created;
> We can start with the Sun, moon, stars, the earth, mankind, plants animals, atoms, molecules, DNA, the Kingdom of GOD, and everything else.
> On God's side of the ledger for daily life:
> God created and supplies air, water, light, plants, and animals.

Are you so arrogant or ego driven to believe God needed you to do whatever work you do? To understand GOD's promise for earthly provision to those, "who seek first the Kingdom", let us look at the provision of the Israelites during their 40-year march to the Promised Land.

> Forgetting The Lord your God - who brought you out of the land of Egypt, where you lived as slaves; who led you through the vast and fearsome desert, with its poisonous snakes, scorpions and waterless, thirsty ground; **who brought water out of flint rock for you; who fed you in the desert with manna,** unknown to your ancestors; all the while humbling and testing you in order to do you good in the end - you will think to yourself, 'My own power and

The Atomic Power of Love, 59

the strength of my own hand have gotten me this wealth.' No, you are to remember your God, because **it is he, GOD, who is giving you the power to get wealth,** in order to confirm his covenant, which he swore to your ancestors, as is happening even today. Deuteronomy 8:16-18

Notice GOD supplied the Manna every morning and the quail in the evening, except the Sabbath but there was work to do to prepare the grain and the birds for eating. The provision we receive will also need to be prepared.

The picture of the Kingdom of GOD is further revealed in the Old Testament when GOD described the Promised Land to the Israelites, it is a picture of GOD's rest and provision. In the new testament this is referred to as entering God's rest.

> "When the Lord your God has brought you into the land he swore to your ancestors Abraham, Isaac, and Jacob that **he would give you** - cities great and prosperous, which **you didn't build;** houses full of all sorts of good things, which **you didn't** fill; water cisterns dug out, which **you didn't dig;** vineyards and olive trees, which **you didn't plant** - and you have eaten your fill; then be careful **not to forget** Your Creator, who brought you out of the land of Egypt, where you lived as slaves. Deuteronomy 6:10-12

Do not miss the opposite of "Thanksgiving" and its penalty.

> Therefore, they have no excuse; because, although they know who God is, **they do not glorify him as God or thank him.** On the contrary, they have become (pointless) futile in their thinking; and their undiscerning hearts have become darkened. **Claiming to be wise, they have become fools!** Romans 1:20-22

Looking at a flower **and knowing in your heart that GOD made that flower** in all its beauty and **giving thanks to GOD** for reminding you of how great is your GOD and how much GOD cares for you is Kingdom living.

> Among you there should not even be mentioned sexual immorality, or any kind of impurity, or greed; these are utterly inappropriate for God's holy people. Also out of place are obscenity and stupid talk

or coarse language; instead, **you should be giving thanks.** Ephesians 5:3

The absolute opposite of Kingdom living are the works of the flesh and coarse language which come from the enemy getting a thought stronghold in a Believer's mind. The evidence will be inappropriate language and an aversion to praising GOD. The Holy Spirit will remind the Believer that the "Finished works of Jesus Christ" include knocking down strongholds, but it is the Believer's choice to resume praising God, honoring GOD, and living in thanksgiving. God gave Believers the world and its beauty and the Holy Spirit to lead Believers into Kingdom living.

GOD said, "It is finished." after creating the world. Let the world produce. Jesus said, "It is finished." When He paid the price for sin. Let the world believe and receive.

When Jesus said, "It is finished" all of the work of redemption and sufficiency was complete. Now God offers Believers
> His Promised land, (rest and sufficiency).
> > Grace replaced the Law.
> > > **Supply replaced demand.**
> > GOD is inside you and
> you are once again teamed up with GOD,
> a super conqueror of your world.

Jesus said, "I AM the Way — and the Truth and the Life; no one comes to the Father **except through me.** John 14:6

This scripture is more comprehensive than the connotation of a first reading. Jesus starts by using:
> The Name for Almighty GOD when Jesus says, **"I am"**
> **"The Way"** referred to in Isaiah 26, The highway to Righteousness.
> **"The Truth"** the perfectness and fulfillment of every aspect of GOD. Perfect Justice, Perfect Grace, Perfect forgiveness, Perfect

redemption.

"The Life" highlighted in Psalms 16:11 Thou wilt shew me the path of life: **in thy presence is fullness of joy; at thy right hand there are pleasures for evermore.**

Can you believe and accept the Lord's way, truth, and life or will you remain depending on your ability, which is never enough? A Believer's ability is important only when motivated by love and faith in GOD.

Believers can experience knowing The Father by living through the Son, joined together with the Spirit.

What does that mean? How do you do it?

The Spiritual world for Believers is straight forward; the who, what, where, when, and how is not complicated, love your GOD and receive GOD's love for you and go about doing good. Remember, "GOD is love "and GOD is His word" living in Christ is to live in love and GOD's word. Abiding with GOD is that easy and this hard. The important question is; **Can Believers get ourselves "out of the way"** to dedicate our efforts to live, love and have our being in relationship with Jesus Christ? If you love GOD and live with GOD, you will be doing what GOD wants you to do, and being what GOD wants you to be. You will automatically, love your neighbor as yourself and you will be the epitome of the Golden rule. **If Believers can grasp who we are and know whose we are; then direction from the Holy Spirit will equip Believers for any situation with wisdom and supernatural power if needed.** This is not to say that this life is without persecution because Jesus promised persecution for Believers. The devils influence is all around you and in most conversations, the opportunity to agree with something unwholesome, to envy, to be in strife, or grow to anger must be arrested and brought to the Lordship of Jesus Christ in your Spirit. Believers will be laughed at and scoffed for believing in a GOD you can't see and talking about life after death. We are promised the victory for the right choice and to stand in faith.

Believers must live in our new Identity
We are sons and daughters of the Creator of All
Our brother Jesus Christ has sent His Spirit to indwell us.

The problem for Believers is controlling wrong influences in a Believer's mind, that if allowed to stay will manifest into actions. Listen to these scriptures for Believers who can keep God in the forefront of their mind and life.

> **Isaiah 26:3** Thou(God) will keep **believers in perfect peace,** whose mind is stayed on GOD: because the believer trusteth in GOD. Trust ye in the LORD forever: for in the LORD JEHOVAH is everlasting strength:
>
> **Philippians 4:6 Don't worry about anything;** on the contrary, make your requests known to God by prayer and petition, with thanksgiving. Then God's rest, passing all understanding, will keep your hearts and minds safe in union with the Messiah, Jesus Christ. In conclusion, brothers, focus your thoughts on what is true, noble, righteous, pure, lovable or admirable, on some virtue or on something praiseworthy.
>
> **1st Thessalonians 5:15** See that none render evil for evil unto any man; but **ever follow that which is good,** both among yourselves, and to all men. Rejoice evermore. Pray without ceasing. **In everything give thanks:** for this is the will of God in Christ Jesus concerning you.

Keeping our minds stayed on GOD means that we must control our minds and bring every thought captive to the Lordship of Jesus Christ. **David believed in GOD** and it was counted for righteousness. Take another look at the 103rd Psalm. Notice that **David commands his mind, will, and soul** to get in line with his belief.

> **Bless the LORD,** O my soul, and all that is within me, **bless his holy name!**
> **Bless the LORD,** O my soul, and **forget not all his benefits,** who forgives all your iniquity,
> > who heals all your diseases,

The Atomic Power of Love, 63

who redeems your life from the pit,
>who crowns you with love and mercy,
who satisfies you with good
so that your youth is renewed like the eagle's.
The LORD works righteousness and justice for all who are oppressed…
Bless the LORD, O my soul!
This is a great look at what a Believer needs to do when the enemy tries to influence a Believer's direction with lies and tries to steal your victory. You are a Child of the Most High GOD, the brother of Jesus Christ, and the Holy Spirit is inside you with your eternal passport and resurrection power. King David's word is still valuable today, "Bless the Lord! O my soul and forget not all GOD's benefits.

GOD's plan is not only to offer salvation,
But it is to bring you into an
Eternal relationship with a Holy GOD, now.

Adam and Eve had a choice to believe a lie or GOD's word and they chose the lie. Now we have a choice to believe GOD's word or a lie and Believers have chosen GOD's word. The result of choosing Jesus Christ is infinitely more valuable than a ticket to Heaven. Sin kept us from the presence of God. **Now Jesus has opened the door to living with the presence of GOD Almighty, Jesus Christ, and the Holy Spirit.** Believers reside and have their being in the life we share with the Holy Spirit in the Kingdom of GOD. The world of the Spirit is not something mystical; it is another dimension to the world we live in, today. Your inner sanctum is an interconnected parallel spiritual life. GOD is available all day every day, not to be worked, but to be loved and to love you in return. The Spiritual realm is available, right now, and you can talk to your Father God, your Brother Jesus, and your friend the Holy Spirit. The power of the Spiritual world is "GOD's Love" and the cornerstone is actions motivated by a word from GOD or from the Bible.

"I believed, and so I spoke," we also believe, and so we also speak,
2nd Corinthians 4:13
The Bible promises are the currency of your inheritance. Most of your inheritance is voice activated and is in your heart waiting on you.

The Atomic Power of Love, 64

What is keeping you from yielding to the free gift of Right standing with Almighty GOD?

Do you know how to receive a gift?

What do you say when someone gives you an unexpected gift?

Is your reply?

Oh no, I can't receive that, I didn't get you anything.

Or I don't deserve this gift.

Do you resist receiving from GOD because you don't have anything to give GOD? **Any of these responses take away from the Grace offered by Jesus Christ,** You cannot earn GOD's Grace. God's plan is not a contest, it is a Covenant, GOD will be your GOD if you yield your right to be your own god. Children of Grace must learn and believe this word: **The battle is the Lord's.**

Adam and Eve chose against GOD and it affected all mankind with a sin nature, **Believers choose GOD** and are eternally welcomed into the Kingdom of GOD. Grace is "the gift" and it is incorruptible! Believers cannot do anything to lose your right standing with GOD because you did not do any work to deserve your righteousness. You were made righteous by Jesus Christ.

> Forasmuch as ye know that **ye were not redeemed** with corruptible things, as silver and gold,...; But with the precious blood of Christ, as of a lamb without blemish and without spot: Who (Jesus) verily was foreordained before the foundation of the world, but was manifest in these last times for you (Believers), 1 Peter 2:18

Love is the ultimate force in GOD's world.

At first, it is difficult to understand the "Concept of abiding in GOD", because we do so many things for ourselves and we do not see, feel, hear, taste, or smell GOD on a daily basis. Therefore, needing GOD is **not** at the top of our list and resting in God **may not** even be on our list. We are so blessed to live in the richest country in the world where a person's basic needs, don't drive Spiritual actions. Hunger, clothing, and shelter are easily obtained within our own power in America. This ease of our daily needs sets up a real impediment to believing in GOD as your provider. GOD is not against rich, smart, well educated people, but don't be misguided into thinking that whatever you do for a business, that you produced the power to get wealth or you will miss the beauty of GOD's love for you.

> As ye have therefore received Christ Jesus the Lord, so walk ye in him: Rooted and built up in him, and established in the faith, as ye have been taught, abounding therein with thanksgiving. **Beware lest any man spoil you through philosophy and vain deceit, after the tradition of men, after the rudiments of the world, and not after Christ.** For in him dwelleth all the fullness of the Godhead bodily. Colossians 2:6-9

What will it take for you to realize who you are and that Almighty GOD is inside Believers to deliver power for accomplishing His will through His Children.

In my own fight to abide in GOD and have God abide in me, I am completely unprepared for catastrophic mortality problems. My life seems wonderful and is wonderful, but I am unprepared for back pain that is debilitating. The pain and the inability to fix the pain place a large speed bump in my world. My Spiritual life is assured so that I can fight a momentary pain problem with an Eternal outcome. I am not having a problem with believing in GOD or resting in GOD, but I am having to reach deep into my heart for strength from My GOD to solve the problem of processing my inability to believe for my healing, which I know was part of the finished works of Jesus Christ and is part of my inheritance as a Believer. Even when the Devil is asking me "Where is your GOD and why don't the scriptures work to heal your body?" Believers **must not** believe the lie of the devil; the enemy always leaves out that death of a Believer's body is the door to complete freedom of our Spirit. Also Believers must remember, the deterioration of our bodies was set in motion by the sin of the world but our New Created life is Eternal and not subject to dying. The best thing that can happen to a Believer is that they die and are instantly with the Lord, but it is better to be fighting the enemy in the name of Jesus Christ as we go to be with the Lord. Satan, the identity thief, will constantly be trying to derail Believer's thinking by the introduction of false choices in your mind to control your thought life instead of Believers depending on GOD Almighty.

Reflecting back after being healed through back surgery, my study has given me another explanation for my inability to appropriate the benefits of Salvation (healing). There are two different aspects to our physical body; one physical deterioration that happens through age (sin being introduced into the world) and one being a lie of the enemy. The Believer has complete control over the Spiritual world and a lie of the enemy being introduced causing sickness or pain, but the physical consequences of our pre-Christian life have not all become new. For example: If part of your old life was gluttony, even if you ae now eating with moderation, your knees, hips, and heart are all damaged from the excess weight. Your new life as a Believer puts you in control of the gluttony as part of your salvation, but you will need a miracle from the Holy Spirit to reverse the effects of deterioration.

Religion and Denominations do not need to set up rules to get good behavior in a person who loves GOD with all his heart and his neighbor as himself. If you "believe" in Salvation through Jesus Christ and rapture to Heaven, what part of supplying your physical needs on earth do you have trouble believing? Religions and Denominations want you to believe that your obedience will make a good spiritual life; **"Do good, get good. Do bad, get bad".** Our Performance is only important if it is motivated by an act of faith in the finished works of Jesus Christ. It is not the Believer's obedience that counts to GOD, it is the obedience of Jesus Christ that gives the Believers mercy and grace. Our position in Jesus Christ is important because our new direction is to live, love, and have our being in Jesus.

Everything about the Believer's spiritual life is a gift. The recipients of GOD's Grace should react to the free gift with praise but the Church has directed Believers into a life of sin-conscious condemnation measured by works, tithing, confession, church attendance, and many other subtle teachings that keep believers living under the law of works instead of the freedom of Grace. The "Freedom " is to not be required to do any requirement, just believe that every single work of Jesus Christ has been finished and allow that belief to result in growth from Faith to Faith. Experience answered prayer and peace growing from our confidence in GOD as we depend on GOD for Daily wellbeing.

Wait a minute, Wait a minute
How can love be the power controlling the universe?

GOD is not constrained by a body and therefore, when we think about our interaction with God, we need to expand our thinking to imagine the Spiritual world. The first step into the Spiritual World is experienced when we enter in prayer, praise, and worship of GOD. God is inside you and omnipresent with Jesus. Enlarge your vision of GOD. When Believers pray and enter into praise you are in the Spiritual world and the Spiritual world is not restrained by your body. You are in God's presence.

To add to the incomprehensible thought of being in the presence of GOD. The other force in the Kingdom of GOD is family. Jesus calls us brothers and sisters and tells us to pray "Our Father". Can you imagine the magnitude of being included in the family of GOD, when you go about your day, **you are never alone.** Start saying and believing that Jesus Christ is our Brother and we can pray to "OUR FATHER." Until Believers begin to accept our new position in Jesus Christ we will not understand that choosing GOD, as our Savior, is the entrance criteria for the new Creation Life. Religion has missed the most important aspect of Salvation, not the ability to live holy but right standing with GOD, on Earth, today, right now. Our new life includes the authority GOD has spoken into Believers and all the benefits of being a child of GOD. And the reason that love powers the entire world is GOD made the Universe and has chosen to abide inside every Believer 24/7.

Believers must not miss exploring
the Spiritual World of our Father, GOD.

The worlds (physical and Spiritual) are powered by building blocks we cannot see; atoms, genes, molecules, spirits and more. In general, Mankind cannot name the Periodic Table of Elements or describe how GOD put atoms and molecules together to make this world operate, or explain the Gene sequencing for the growth of your body from conception to maturity. And the structure of the Spiritual Universe may not have crossed the Believer's mind, but your "Right now"," Abundant", "Eternal" life is part of the Spiritual world and it is available now. The Spiritual world will never be completely realized without the knowledge of GOD and the diligent pursuit of the Kingdom of GOD and His Righteousness. When Believers know "who they are?" and "whose they are?" they will reign over all the lies of the Identity thief and be able to eliminate strife filled situations.

All Power and Authority
is in the control of
Jesus Christ

Read carefully this scripture from Hebrews.
GOD, Hath in these last days spoken unto us by his Son,
        whom he hath appointed heir of all things,
                by whom also he made the worlds;
                        Who being the brightness of his glory, and
                                the express image of his person, and
                        upholding all things by the word of his power,
                when he had by himself purged our sins,
        sat down on the right hand of the Majesty on high; Hebrews 1:2-3
Notice that the power and authority that powers all the worlds is upheld by Jesus Christ and Believers are part of the Lord's Family and have been given authority to use GOD's power.

Answer this;
Jesus possessed all power to heal, forgive sins, walk on water, resurrect the dead, and yet HE prayed all the time.
        Did Jesus pray to have the power to bless people with miracles or did Jesus have the power to do miracles because he prayed?
        Or did the Lord's prayers develop such a relationship with the Father, that doing GOD's will was all Jesus wanted to do? And when doing GOD's will the power happens for the needs of the

Lord's neighbors because it is GOD's will?

For the Believer;

> **When your heart** is sold out to the Father and you are immersed in the Father, the actions motivated by perfect love, are perfect,
>
> **And everything you touch** or come near is blessed and made whole because your actions are born out of love and service and in the will of Almighty God.

A relationship with Jesus Christ and attention to his words allow believers to expect to do greater things than Jesus did because GOD is now inside us, which is more powerful than when He was with us in a Physical Body. The scripture says When Jesus ascends to Heaven, He will send the Holy Spirit a "comforter". The word "comforter" is a confusing term and we have missed the power of a relationship with Almighty GOD by allowing the connotation of the word "comforter" to mean Believers need a shoulder to cry upon. The comfort comes from the exchange of GOD "with us" in Human form, to Christians becoming the Holy of Holies and GOD living inside us!!! Believers are all extensions of God on earth. You can be The Temple for indwelling of Almighty GOD and have resurrection power inside you, and not know what the power is or how to activate it. You must read the will to see what you have inherited from Jesus.

> Hebrews 11:3 Through faith we understand that the worlds were framed by the word of God, **so that things which are seen were not made of things which do appear.**
>
> 2nd Corinthians 4:18 While we look **not** at the things which are seen, but at the things which are **not** seen: for the things which are seen are temporal; **but the things which are not seen are eternal.**

Everything about your Spiritual life has been given to you as a Gift; from Jesus, The Father, and The Holy Spirit, when Believers follow the leading of the Spirit and become a giver of gifts of love we perfect the love God has given us and the Glory from those gifts glorifies Jesus and the Father. This is not an exercise in trying to live Holy; it is a commitment to believe right, leading to living right. There is never anything wrong with doing right, but when the motivation to do right, springs forth from loving GOD, it has spiritual significance.

People don't go to Hell as judgment for their sin they go to hell for rejecting Jesus Christ. People don't go to Heaven because of their works Believers go to Heaven because their family lives there.

Chapter 4

Love is not a virtue of Mankind
It is a virtue of Godkind
Believers are children of the Supernatural.

As we travel through the stages of learning about Jesus Christ and change the direction of our thoughts and find that part of GOD that is inside Believers, we must continue renewing our minds, but with a different view, direction, or agenda in mind. Believers are no longer trying to become a new creature without a sin to our name, we are a new creation, we are now seated with Jesus in Heaven, we are now the fruit of the work of Jesus and each Believer is our Lord's gift of glory to the Father.

> But when one turns to the Lord, the veil is removed. Now the Lord is the Spirit, and where the Spirit of the Lord is, there is freedom. And we all, with unveiled face, beholding the glory of the Lord, are being transformed into the same image from one degree of glory to another. For this comes from the Lord who is the Spirit 2nd Corinthians 3:16-18.

Unbelief denies entry to GOD's Grace,
Belief guards the availability of GOD's Grace

Now Believers must learn how to act in the Spiritual realm where we are omnipresent with Jesus. The Eternal Believer is not what they feel emotionally but the Believer is what they believe. Our inner sanctum is filled with the Holy Spirit, we are filled with an active relationship with GOD, and that connection is available to reign in life. In this realm, actions **are not as important** as the belief from which an action was motivated. At the most basic motivation there is only evil leading to death or good leading to GOD. Believers have a significant role to play in doing God's will on Earth as it is in Heaven. Through the love of GOD "Believers can do **all things.**"

Holiness is a reference to GOD's perfectness, Every aspect of GOD is perfect and is separated from failure,

The Believer's right standing with GOD is perfect. The perfectness of Jesus sacrifice has made Believers Holy (separated to God), forever. What does this mean? Holiness is being separated because of the aspects of perfectness. GOD is referred to as "Holy, Holy, Holy" bringing perspective to the perfectness of each aspect of his character and being. When we believe our need for GOD and receive GOD's gift of righteousness (Jesus) and His love, we receive his perfectness, **not that we are perfect but that GOD's Gift of His love is perfect.** From that time forward our knowledge of the FACT that GOD Almighty Loves Believers separates us into GOD's beloved. Then we can shout from the rooftops I am the one GOD loves or I am GOD's beloved!! GOD did not sacrifice his son for you and give you a new life in right standing with Himself to see you condemned, cursed, impoverished, or diseased.

> Jesus said, the thief cometh not, but for to steal, and to kill, and to destroy: I am come that they (Believers) might have life, and that they might have it more abundantly. John 10:10

How does our new life in Jesus Christ change our actions to live in the abundant life and shun the enemy who is trying to kill, steal, and destroy Believers? Believers must know their identity, "Who you are." to trust the power of GOD indwelling the Believer.

With GOD's perfectness "we can do all things" Actions we have not conceived are in our ability.

Outside the Perfect love of Jesus Christ, we can do "no thing" John 15:5. Listen to the Love story in the following three parables and words of GOD. GOD created the world and gave it to mankind and it did not produce good fruit. But the Gardner has planted a new vine, with a different root system and it produces perfect fruit.

Isaiah 5:1 I want to sing a song for someone I love, a song about my loved one and his vineyard. My loved one had a vineyard on a very fertile hill. He dug up its stones and cleared them away, planted it with the choicest vines, built a watchtower in the middle of it, and carved out in its rock a winepress. He expected it to produce good grapes, but it produced only sour, wild grapes. "Now, citizens of Jerusalem (Israel) and people of Judah (Gentiles), judge between me and my vineyard. What more could I have done for my vineyard that I haven't already done in it? **So why,** when I expected good grapes, did it produce sour, wild grapes?

The story of what the religious men did to the Messiah and to GOD's vineyard.

Matthew 21:33 "Now listen to another parable. There was a farmer who planted a vineyard. He put a wall around it, dug a pit for the winepress and built a tower; then he rented it to tenants and left. When harvest-time came, he sent his servants to the tenants to collect his share of the crop. But the tenants seized his servants — this one they beat up, that one they killed, another they stoned. So he sent some other servants, more than the first group, and they did the same to them. Finally, he sent them his son, saying, 'My son they will respect.' But when the tenants saw the son, they said to each other, 'This is the heir. Come, let's kill him and take his inheritance!' So they grabbed him, threw him out of the vineyard and killed him. Now when the owner of the vineyard comes, what will he do to those tenants?" They answered him, "He will viciously destroy those vicious men and rent out the vineyard to other tenants who will give him His share of the crop when it's due." Jesus said to them, "Haven't you ever read in the Bible, 'The very rock which the builders rejected has become the cornerstone! This has come from the Lord, and in our eyes it is amazing'? Therefore, I tell you that the Kingdom of God will be taken away from you and given to the kind of people that will produce its fruit!"

The Body of Christ
is having an Identity crisis.

Understanding Believer's new life in the Vine which is rooted in Jesus Christ and pruned by Father GOD, Believers are the branches and we get to bear or display the fruit. Believers **did not make** the fruit, prepare the soil, or build the winepress, the gardener and the root which is the vine made the fruit, Believers are the branches that display what Jesus Christ, our Messiah has done. Listen to the explanation of the parable by Jesus.

John 15:1 "I am the real vine, and my Father is the gardener. Every branch which is part of me but fails to bear fruit, he cuts off; and every branch that does bear fruit, he prunes, so that it may bear more fruit. Right now, because of the word which I have spoken to you, you are pruned. Stay united with me, as I will with you — for just as the branch can't put forth fruit by itself apart from the vine, so you can't bear fruit apart from me. "I am the vine and you are the branches. Those who stay united with me, and I with them, are the ones who bear much fruit; because apart from me you can do nothing. Unless a person remains united with me, he is thrown away like a branch and dries up. Such branches are gathered and thrown into the fire, where they are burned up. **"If you remain united with me, and my words with you, then ask whatever you want, and it will happen for you. This is how my Father is glorified — in your bearing much fruit; this is how you will prove to be my disciples.** "Just as my Father has loved me, I too have loved you; so stay in my love. If you keep my commands, you will stay in my love — just as I have kept my Father's commands and stay in his love. I have said this to you so that my joy may be in you, and your joy may be complete. **"This is my command: that you keep on loving each other just as I have loved you.** No one has greater love than a person who lays down his life for his friends. You are my friends, if you do what I command you. Love each other as I have loved you is the command.

The invisible world controls the visible world.

Now, Believers must learn how to live in the only realm where we are omnipresent with Jesus. With the indwelling of the Holy Spirit, Believers are filled with an active relationship with GOD, our Spirit is made in the image of GOD and in covenant with GOD Almighty. **In this invisible realm of the Spirit, actions are not as important as the belief from which an action was motivated.** GOD is love and love is the will of God and serving others with the love of God is the essence of what GOD wanted the world to experience and it will. The lamb will lie down with the lion and the carnivore will eat grass with the cow, the child will play by the hole of the snake, and the roses will have no thorns. Consider the enormity of this change from evil to love necessary to restructure GOD's created world. This is the invisible realm where Peter said bid me to come walk on the water, Jesus said come, and Peter walked on the water, he began to sink when he considered that the wind was great and the waves were high. Jesus reached out to Peter and they walked to the boat and then through the power of the invisible Spiritual world the disciples and the boat were translated to the other side of the lake instantly. The love in the invisible spiritual world is powerful to affect the seen world.

Beware
Believers can have a hard heart. (unbelief)

Faith is power for effective prayer and is part of a relationship with GOD and forms our belief system. The "mustard seed" promise in Matthew 17:20 does not refer to the size of the demon the disciples were trying to cast out but was a description of the unbelief that caused doubt in the disciple's heart. The faith necessary to control the demon, only needed to be the size of a mustard seed if planted in the heart of a Believer, **but not in the heart of unbelief.** At this time the Disciples had Jesus with them in body, but not abiding in them. A hard heart is still a problem for Believers, the self-sufficiency that is a part of the world, separates us from receiving the gifts of life with Almighty GOD.

A Believer has faith or belief that your car will start, or the chair will hold your weight, but what can you definitively say you have faith for in the Spiritual world? Jesus said Believers would do greater works than He has done because he was sending the Holy Spirit to indwell Believers. Have you experienced any of the works of Jesus in your life? Unless you are very unusual I have thrown a wrench in your belief system and your relationship with GOD.

> Verily, verily, I say unto you, He that believeth on me, the works that I do shall he do also; and greater works than these shall he do; because I go unto my Father. And whatsoever ye shall ask in my name, that will I do, that the Father may be glorified in the Son. John 14:12-13

Note; Prayer is not always in a private place, or on your knees, or in worship, but can also be in speaking GODs word to affect the seen world with the power of GOD's love from the unseen world of the Spirit. Your relationship with GOD is as fully developed as you make it. Guarantee; A Believer will never be happier than when he or she is consumed by interaction with GOD Almighty.

Believers must Believe
That God is inside your body with your Spirit.

GOD is in the Spiritual realm; a Believer must be in the Spiritual realm to interact with GOD. Now when we hear, **seek ye first the Kingdom of GOD and His Righteousness** and all these things shall be added unto you, now this Spiritual world takes on a new dimension. **It is where GOD is** and Believers are welcome to enter. If you enter you will find GOD's rest (total wellbeing).

> "The Lord is my Shepherd **and I shall not want.**" Psalms 23

As a Believer "How magnificent is your GOD?" It is up to the level you believe.

The relationship we have with GOD is our faith basis for the promise of Matthew 7:7 (that if you ask and seek, you will find) and this depends on our confidence (faith) in the heavenly Father. The Disciples after seeing Jesus walk on the water, calm the storm, translate the boat to the other side of the lake and feed the five thousand, instantly, were assessed to have a hard heart or unbelief.

> Mark 6:50 For they all saw him, and were troubled. And

immediately he talked with them, and saith unto them, Be of good cheer: it is I; be not afraid. And he went up unto them into the ship; and the wind ceased: and they were sore amazed in themselves beyond measure, and wondered. **For they considered not the miracle of the loaves: for their heart was hardened.**

Mark 8:16 Jesus said, "Why are you talking with each other about having no bread? **Don't you see or understand yet? Have your hearts been made like stone?** You have eyes — don't you see? You have ears — don't you hear? And don't you remember? When I broke the five loaves for the five thousand, how many baskets full of broken pieces did you collect?" Twelve," they answered him.

Matthew 13:15 For this people's **heart is waxed gross** (hardened), and their ears are dull of hearing, and their eyes they have closed; lest at any time they should see with their eyes, and hear with their ears, and should understand with their heart, and should be converted, and I should heal them.

GOD did not bring you out of the world of Sin to lock you in the dungeon of lack, sickness, anxiety, and darkness.

Now when we read, "GOD is LOVE", Believers have the criteria from which to evaluate and capture negative thoughts. Now the motivation of each thought and action is "the drama in your life", will you as a Believer bring "every thought" captive to the Lordship of Jesus Christ? Now Believers can begin to understand the scriptures;

If ye abide in me, and my words abide in you, ye shall ask what ye will, and it shall be done unto you. John 15:7

And from the Lord's Prayer, "Thy Kingdom come thy will be done on Earth as it is in Heaven" from Matthew 6,

Beloved friends, let us love one another; because love is from God; and everyone who "loves" has God as his Father and knows God. Those who do not "love", do not know God; because "God is love". Here is how God showed his love among us: God sent his only Son into the world, so that through him we might have life. **Here is what love** is: not that we have loved God, but that he loved us and sent his Son to be the propitiation for our sins. **Beloved friends, if this is how God loved us, we likewise ought to love one another.** 1st John 4

It's not your actions that made you righteous, it is a Believer's believing and even that action was a gift. A Believer's need for supernatural help will manifest when a Believer has a word from GOD and compassion for the situations.

Contemplate the fact, that
Perfect "love "cast out fear. 1st John 1:18
What other aspects of life does" Perfect Love" control?
GOD is love and
when we abide in Love we are in the will of GOD,
doing the will of GOD and
bearing much fruit
giving away the "LOVE" given us.
There is no fear in your Spirit because GOD is there.
The Lord has not given you a Spirit of fear
but a Spirit of Love,
a Spirit of Power and
a Spirit of a Sound Mind.
II Timothy 1:7

A Believer's faith can appropriate all the benefits of Salvation and the promises in GOD's word that further GOD's will on Earth as it is in Heaven. Unfortunately for Believers, your ability to appropriate the power of the Spiritual world through Love is based on your belief in GOD and His Spiritual world. Belief and faith grow by learning the word of GOD and meditation and communication with the Holy Spirit. If you believe GOD is inside you and given you power to reign in life you will reign, if you don't believe, it will not happen for you.

Questions to promote thought.

Question; If you can rightly divide the word of GOD, can you wrongly divide the word of God? Listen to this verse from 2nd Timothy 2:15-16

> Study to shew thyself approved unto God, a workman that needeth not to be ashamed, **rightly dividing the word of truth.** But shun profane and vain babblings: for they will increase unto more ungodliness.

Question; Is there evidence, when a Believer is being influenced by the devil and is the evidence "Strife" in a Believer's thoughts and actions?

> But if you **harbor in your hearts bitter jealousy and selfish ambition,** don't boast and attack the truth with lies! This wisdom is not the kind that comes down from above; on the contrary, **it is worldly, unspiritual, demonic.** For where there are jealousy and selfish ambition, there will be disharmony (strife) and every foul practice. James 3:14-16

Question; Were the Lord's prayers, while on Earth, a request for power to do signs that people would believe, or were the prayers an intimate communication with His Father and the intimate relationship of Man and GOD led to great miracles? or was the Lord's relationship with the Father so encompassing that their communication was that of praise and love and the miracles came from the power of a love relationship with GOD?

The "love" that filled Christ's life was the power to do the acts of kindness, we call miracles.

> When Peter and Paul said to the lame man, "We have no money but such as we have, give us to you, RISE up and walk".

Did they give the lame man the "Love" of GOD they had received or was this evidence of the power of the scripture, and their relationship with GOD?

> Ephesians 4:29 Let no corrupt communication proceed out of your mouth, but that which is good to the use of edifying, **that it may minister grace unto the hearers.**
>
> John 1:16 For from his fullness we have all received, **grace upon grace.**
>
> For the law was given through Moses; **grace and truth came through Jesus Christ. John 1:17**

The scriptures are saying that we can speak grace from our mouths and that its effect can be ministry of healing. Jesus is a person and **Grace and truth came with Him.** Grace is GOD's action to his love for Mankind.

> And the Word became flesh and dwelt among us, and we have seen his glory, glory as of the only Son from the Father, **full of grace and truth.** John 1:14

The concept of loving GOD with all your heart
Is difficult in a world
Full of work and false accomplishments.

There is never anything wrong with doing right.
Everyone knows the story of the broken covenant between Adam, Eve, and GOD with the resulting release of the knowledge of evil and good, resulting in the curse of the earth, mankind, and Satan. For 6000 plus years, we have lived in a world of evil **without having embraced the knowledge and acts of goodness.**
In the natural or Earthly realm of living; "doing good" does not have a positive visible effect on the giver of good but inures to the benefit of the receiver.
What is the motivation, for an act of kindness that would cause Believers to do good for others without adding to their prosperity or the wellbeing of the doer? Can there be a positive effect on the doer of goodness? What possible positive effect can there be on giving some of your valuable substance away resulting in a reduction of your own prosperity? **GOD's system is exactly opposite to the constant march toward storing up things to add to a Believer's material prosperity.** If you could take anything with you into life after the death of your body, accumulating wealth would be important. In contrast, you can only take your good deeds done in love.

These questions exemplify the problem of "What is mankind's purpose?" and "Why are we here?" and "Why did GOD set up such a system that does not make sense to the natural mind of mankind?" In the Spiritual world, doing good for others stores up treasures in Heaven and is multiplied and given back to the giver on Earth. Look at the scriptures about Joseph and the power of having a relationship with GOD.

> Gen 39:2 And the LORD was with Joseph, and he was a prosperous man; and he was in the house of his master the Egyptian. And his master saw that the LORD was with him, and that the LORD made all that he did to prosper in his hand. And Joseph found grace in his sight, and he served him: and he made him overseer over his house, and all that he had he put into his hand. And it came to pass from the time that he had made him overseer in his house, and over all that he had, that the LORD blessed the Egyptian's house for Joseph's sake; and the blessing of the LORD was upon all that he had in the house, and in the field.

Going forward into more of the knowledge of Good and acts of kindness, Jesus has given us an example that unlocks some of the answers we have to GOD's Spiritual World. Examine the result of the Lord's act of kindness to believers.

Jesus became sin
> **who knew no sin and**
>> **we were made righteous**
>>> **when we did nothing right.**

If GOD treated Jesus like the greatest sinner ever and
> **treats you and I as the most righteous person ever.**
>> **We should receive GOD's love and**
>>> **Rejoice.**

The "Truth" Believers must integrate into our lives is **GOD owns the world and everything in the world;**

> Believers must adjust to "the truth" that if we give something away, we are NOT going to have less. Our gift was not ours when we gave it away, it was GOD's.

> Believers work to be successful, and that is God's plan, but we must never forget that it is GOD who gives us the power to get wealth.

> A Believer's success, "that yields pride", will bring with it "fear of losing" what a Believer considers his own.

When Believers understand "who they are" and "who GOD is" Believers can dedicate their lives to loving GOD and receiving GOD's love and going about doing good and know that GOD is our source and giving away some of our substance is like planting a seed that produces an even larger harvest.

Philosophy
Wrong philosophy will yield wrong conclusions
Colossians 2:8
Wrong conclusions lead to wrong thinking,
Wrong thinking leads to wrong emotions
Wrong emotions lead to wrong feelings,
Wrong feelings lead to wrong actions,
Wrong actions lead to bad results.

Chapter 5

Where and what is the invisible world of the Spirit? "The Questions" Not answered by our religion today.

Grace has not set you free to sin, but free from sin!
Believers no longer have a sin nature; there is only one sin that is held to your account, "Do you believe in Jesus Christ?" **Unbelief cannot be forgiven** because it is unbelief in GOD. When Believers choose to exchange being their "own god and supplier" for a relationship with Almighty GOD and His sufficiency, then Adam's sin is reversed and a Believer's Spirit is born again.

Now Believers must move to understand the Spiritual world of their Eternal life and renew our mind so that Believers can comprehend more about our Born-again Spirit. This New Eternal life is not referring to after we die in the sweet by and by, but NOW. Confirmed by John 3:16, 1st John 4:12-16, Colossians 3:1-5 or Romans 14:17, Jeremiah 9:23-25 and many more.

Believers must **learn to measure time by eternity,** and to weigh the value of earthly things by the mortality of your body.

> If a Believer is going to live forever, why be bothered by a situation that is here today and gone tomorrow.
> If a Believer's body is going to die and we cannot bring any earthly treasure with us into Heaven, don't be overcome by storing up treasure.
> If Believers believe God owns everything then being a giver cannot hurt the giver because it was not the Believer's, when it was given.
> If Believers are going to live forever with GOD Almighty, why worry about tomorrow.

The totality of your earthly fortune cannot be compared to what you now have with GOD inside you. GOD owns the universe. Believers must explore and find our Spiritual world and develop our relationship with the Holy Spirit who owns the physical world and the Spiritual world. Do not forget that there are laws that govern the Spiritual world just as evident as gravity.

Abraham was searching,

> "For he looked for a city which hath foundations, whose builder and maker is God" (Hebrews 11:10).
>
> And God blessed his trust, He had "believed God, and it was counted unto him for righteousness" (Romans 4:3).

Believers don't have to search for the Spiritual Kingdom which foundations are made by GOD, because the Temple made without hand is inside Believers.

Contemplate this scripture from Acts. How do we accomplish this?

In HIM (Jesus) we live, love and have our being. Acts 17:28

Our new covenant is to Love GOD and to receive GOD's love for us. Again we are being told to have our "being" in beholding our Savior and loving others as our lifestyle. God is a Spirit so we must find our Spiritual self to be able to have our being in Jesus Christ. To engage with Jesus, Believers must communicate both with our voices and in the Spirit. Believers must also try to move our mind and body under the control of our Spirit, because our Spirit is perfect and joined with the Holy Spirit, this influence from perfection will manifest actions in the will of GOD.

> **In him** we have redemption through his blood, the forgiveness of our trespasses, according to the riches of his grace, which he lavished upon us, in all wisdom and insight making known to us the mystery of his will, according to his purpose, which he set forth in Christ as a plan for the fullness of time, **to unite all things in him, things in heaven and things on earth. In him** we have obtained an inheritance, having been predestined according to the purpose of him who works all things according to the counsel of his will, so that we who were the first to hope **in Christ** might be to the praise of his glory. **In him** you also, when you heard the word of truth, the gospel of your salvation, and believed in him, were sealed with the promised Holy Spirit, Ephesians 1:7-13

Believers must not allow outside influences to divert the power, the passion and the fulfillment of GOD's purpose of uniting things on Earth with things in Heaven.

Consider this analogy;

When a Believer is in an airplane and going at 500 miles per hour at 30,000 feet above the ground; you are going where the plane is going in the power of the plane. **When Jesus is in Believers and Believers are in Jesus you, can walk in the Spirit** and you can use the power of Jesus finished works to unite a Believer's Spirit with the will of GOD on Earth.

> The Lord's Prayer and the first line "Our Father which art in Heaven" is so ingrained in Christians that understanding that the prayer was given before Jesus went to the cross and after the Cross GOD through the Holy Spirit is inside Believers, is difficult to process. **The TRUTH is GOD is inside Believers** and Father God and Jesus are in Heaven.

The power of the New Covenant is activated by Believers through the power of the Spirit. GOD is not coming down from Heaven to help you because GOD is inside you. Listen to this verse from Romans 8:11

> If the Spirit of him who raised Jesus from the dead dwells in you, he who raised Christ Jesus from the dead will also give life to your mortal bodies **through his Spirit who dwells in you**.

Questions Religion has not finished answering "How do we find and live in the Spiritual world?"

The answers to this questions and others is not "How can you accomplish the answers to these questions?" but **"How can you believe that God abides in you and you abide in GOD?"** The following questions have troubled Religion for 2,000 years. The foundation of the worlds Christian churches have not been able to explain the scriptures and God's plan because the trajectory of mankinds attempt to explain GOD's Spiritual world was slightly off target.

For example:

What do we do with this intense love from Almighty GOD? Ephesians 2:4

How can Christ live in me? Galatians 2:20

How can Believers be crucified with Jesus and yet live? Galatians 2:20

How can I be a new creation? II Corinthians 5:17

How do I use the Faith "of" Jesus Christ? Galations 2:20

How can we be seated with Christ in Heavenly places? Ephesians 2:6

The Atomic Power of Love, 86

To further the discussion,
> **How can we be A NEW CREATION, "now" while we are on earth, when our bodies are old?**
> **And How can our old things be passed away and yet our body is not changed?**

Everything about our existence on Earth will die and be dissolved into dust except The "New life" born again in our bodies. There is a part of the Believer's Spiritual realm that is omnipresent with Jesus Christ, right now. The Bible says so, "If you abide in me and I abide in you". BELIEVING IS NOT EASY because Believers have to change (repent) the entire direction of their mindset from depending on themselves to believing in an invisible GOD. A GOD who loves Believers and wants to serve, protect, love, and supply all our needs. The problem comes with **believing.** A Believer's mind, will, and emotions has **no idea how to make this change. Listen to the instruction from Matthew about living.**
> Therefore **take no thought,** saying,
>> What shall we eat? or,
>>> What we shall drink? or,
>>>> Wherewithal shall we be clothed?
>>>> For after all these things do the unbelievers seek:
>>> for your heavenly Father knoweth
>> that ye have need of all these things.

But seek ye first the kingdom of God, and his righteousness; and all these things shall be added unto you. Matthew 6

Believers do not have a mechanism for "taking no thought" for their necessities of existence or "**seeking first** the Kingdom of GOD" and His Righteousness. What does this mean and how do you do it? **Answer;** Until Believers understand where GOD is and how to get to this Spiritual world, our life trajectory is incomplete. GOD gave Believers authority and instructions to subdue the world. The scripture says, **seek first,** so we can understand the priority of our time, **second** we know that the Holy Spirit has been sent to us to reveal the deep things of GOD, so we have direction, and **third,** we have GOD's word to study for answers. Believers will be in the Kingdom of GOD when by faith a Believer is seeking GOD,

The Atomic Power of Love, 87

communicating with the Holy Spirit, and meditating and studying the Bible. Believers, when believing, are in the Kingdom of GOD.

Believers must seek God and yield our ability to produce our sufficiency to GOD. Believing God to supply sufficiency for our life does not mean quit working. When GOD sent manna to Israel in the desert, the manna had to be prepared.
This does not mean Believes should quit work.

> In the beginning, at the Believer's point of belief, in Jesus Christ
> we feel the conviction of our sins by the Holy Spirit and
> **trust** in, the gift of grace of Jesus Christ and
> we enter the Spiritual Kingdom of Almighty GOD,
> **but at that point most Believers are a confused mess.**

The mental hurdle, Believers have to jump, is from being Mankind to **GODkind.**

I am not saying that you are GOD, but I am saying that your Spirit is made in the image of GOD and resides in a temple, not made with hands, inside Believers with the Holy Spirit, who is GOD. If you will join your spirit and the Holy Spirit to lead your mind, will, and emotions in a better direction than you can do by yourself, then right believing will produce right living. You don't have to study the bible to transform your mind but it is the easiest way I have found. When a Believer can unite the Spirit and the mind through a word from GOD then the seen world will be changed by the Spiritual world. **When Jesus said, "It is finished." The works of right standing with God and all His Promises were completed and available for Believers.** Jesus is not going to die again to help mankind, His dying is "finished". Listen to Paul in Ephesians 1:14-23

> The **eyes of your understanding being enlightened;** that ye may know what is the hope of his calling, and what the riches of the glory of his inheritance in the saints, And what is the exceeding greatness of his power to us-ward **who believe,** according to the working of his mighty power, Which he wrought in Christ, when he raised him from the dead, and set him at his own right hand in the heavenly places, Far above all principality, and power, and might, and dominion, and every name that is named, not only in

this world, but also in that which is to come: **And hath put all THINGS under his feet, and gave him TO BE the head over all THINGS to the church, Which is his body, the fullness of him that filleth all in all.**

When you are baptized in the Holy Spirit, GOD is in residence with your Spirit all day every day, but it is up to believers to interact and benefit from the power of God available to participate in your every situation.

.

Faith filled words and actions
Are part of the Spiritual Kingdom

The finished works of Jesus are "Finished Works" and the Holy Spirit is inside Believers available to enact the promises of the Bible using the authority given to Believers. **Believers have to believe in their authority and act on the promises of GOD to see them manifest.** Instead of reaching out to God, in Heaven, Believers need to speak from the Spirit who is connected with GOD inside Believers. A Believer must know the promises and act on them. Listen to Paul describe a way of living for Believers in Colossians 3:15-18

> And **above all these put on love, which binds everything together in perfect harmony.** And let the peace of Christ rule in your hearts, to which indeed you were called in one body. And be thankful. Let the word of Christ dwell in you richly, teaching and admonishing one another in all wisdom, singing psalms and hymns and spiritual songs, with thankfulness in your hearts to God. And whatever you do, **in word or deed**, do everything in the name of the Lord Jesus, giving thanks to God, the Father, through him.

Paul, The Apostle details the ingredients in a successful Christian life.

A Believer gets to choose what he or she feeds their Spirit and their body, the physical food will temporarily nourish the body, the food we feed our Spirit will build trust in God and will expand our faith to believe in GOD's provision.

> It is written, Man shall not live by bread alone, but by every word that proceedeth out of the mouth of God. Matthew 4:4

Only when Believers realize the inadequacy of living without GOD and want to live in the Spiritual Kingdom do we ask ourselves, "What do I do now? ", then Believers begin to study, pray, and meditate and find direction from our Lord. The first part of the answer is, seeking GOD will produce peace and provision through **"trusting" GOD.** Our needs will be a product of our work given to us by GOD. If you **don't believe** God will supply you with any particular need **you will be correct,** it will not happen.

> **If you don't believe** that GOD Almighty created the worlds you can see, feel, and touch; are you confident that GOD made Heaven for you which you cannot see, feel, or touch?
>
> GOD loved you so much that he gave his only Son to die for your sins.
>
> **If you don't believe** in an Eternal GOD, can you believe in eternal life after the death of your body?
>
> John 3:18 **He that believeth on him (Jesus) is not condemned** but he that **believeth not** is condemned already, because he hath not believed in the name of the only begotten Son of God.

Unbelief is the only sin that cannot be forgiven because an unbeliever doesn't believe in GOD. The test for believing in GOD is simple; "When you look at this world, do you believe GOD created this world?" Do you believe GOD loves you? Do you believe Jesus died for your sin? Anything less than an unequivocal "yes I believe." confirms you are an unbeliever. Fortunately, it is never too late to choose to believe in Jesus. Listen to this scripture in Colossians,

> For it pleased the Father that in him (Jesus) should all fullness dwell; And, **having made peace through the blood of his cross, by him to reconcile all things unto himself;** by him, I say, whether they be things in earth, or things in heaven. And you, that were sometime **alienated and enemies in your mind by wicked works,** yet now hath he reconciled In the body of his flesh through death, **to present you holy and unblameable and unreproveable in his sight:** If ye continue in the faith grounded and settled, and be not moved away from the hope of the gospel, which ye have heard, and which was preached to every creature which is under heaven;. Even the mystery which hath been hid from ages and from generations, but now is made manifest to his saints: To whom God

would make known what is the riches of the glory of this mystery among the Gentiles; **which is Christ in you, the hope of glory:** Whom we preach, warning every man, and teaching every man in all wisdom; **that we may present every man perfect in Christ Jesus**: Colossians 1:19-28

So the ever-present question is "Can you believe in GOD's love for your Eternal life, your World, and your daily needs?" When Believers begin to believe and speak to the world about our GOD, and his love for Mankind we will change the physical world from the power of the Spiritual world.

The development of "Trust" in the new life in Christ Jesus is up to the time table Believers choose. GOD will allow us to go as slow or fast as a Believer wants in learning to **"Trust in the Believer's inheritance"**. For every step you take to move closer to GOD, GOD will match your movement toward you. You don't have to go to college to learn about **trusting** and drawing near to God, but you must have a relationship with GOD and seek knowledge of what God has for you. Believers cannot inherit and use what you don't know exists and you must weigh the value of earthly things by the discernment of your Spirit.

Jesus died for your sins 2,000 + years ago
Everything Jesus did for you was
"Finished" at Calvary
The Spiritual life and power is inside the Believer.

The seed of Salvation is stocked with the fruit of the Spirit, it is inside a Believer's spirit, and can be summoned. Joy, peace faith, self-control, and the other fruit of the Spirit can be controlled by the Believer, it is inside you, it is yours. Your Spirit and the Holy Spirit is interconnected with your mind and by faith can choose to control your emotions and actions through the power of the Spirit.

For example: In Romans 12:2 This renewing of the mind is the interaction of the new Creation Spirit, Word of GOD, and the Holy Spirit influencing a Believer's mind. Faith in the direction from the Lord will produce actions through summoning a fruit of the Spirit and using it to act in the will of

GOD toward a situation.

For a simple example; A Believer, when frustrated with a long line, can summon peace for the situation and it will come and the Believer will have control over his thoughts. Make sure to slow down, listen, and follow the leading of the Holy Spirit to affect the seen world with power from the Spiritual world. Believers asking the Holy Spirit for direction and power in all situations in daily life will receive leading from the Holy Spirit prompting actions that are in the will of GOD.

> 1st Corinthians 2:12 Now we have received, not the spirit of the world, **but the spirit which is of God; that we might know the things that are freely given to us of God.** Which things also we speak, not in the words which man's wisdom teacheth, but which the Holy Ghost teacheth; comparing spiritual things with spiritual. But the natural man receiveth not the things of the Spirit of God: for they are foolishness unto him: neither can he know them, **because they are spiritually discerned.**

Believers must unplug from the demands of the world and plug into the Spirit of Life in Christ Jesus, it is inside you. Will you accept and believe in your righteousness? The Holy Spirit will lead you into the depths of the gifts GOD has for you **but you have to ask, seek, and knock. GOD wants to be a part of every part of your life.**

We are GOD's Beloved.
Can you picture the Love GOD has for you?

We must employ some new thinking!

Can you recall to your mind; a picture of your first bicycle, car, high School graduation, your first love, your first home, your first cell phone? Now can you picture in your mind the day you accepted Lord Jesus Christ as your Savior, His love for you, His sacrifice for you, the power and authority that is yours because of His sacrifice? Do you have a picture in your mind of GOD's gifts to you? Can you imagine that GOD loves you and made this world for you, so that you could live and breathe; eat and grow and have a relationship with the Creator of All? Can you imagine being made in the image of GOD and Jesus as your older brother? If you cannot imagine then you must concentrate on filling your mind with pictures of GOD's gifts,

The Atomic Power of Love, 92

GOD's love, and GOD's sacrifice for Believers.

Have you allowed your daily existence To dominate your thought life and Given God your left overs?

Don't allow the mental pictures that dominate your mind to be worldly but put pictures in your mind of the grandeur of your God and His love for you. Do not let anyone tell you that you are an old sinner saved by grace with a ticket to heaven. **You are a Believer in right standing with GOD Almighty, indwelt by the Holy Spirit, and in Jesus you live and love and have your being. Right now.**

Jesus died for our sins past, present, and future.
Jesus redeemed us from the curse of the law.   Galatians 3:13
Jesus fulfilled the law.   Matthew 5:17
There is now no condemnation to those who walk
after the Spirit.   Romans 8:1
GOD condemned the sin in the flesh.   Romans 8:3
Believers are now seated with Jesus in Heavenlies. Ephesians 2:6
Believers are now new creations.   II Corinthians 5:17
Almighty God lives inside you.   Galatians 3:20
GOD has designed works for you to do.   Ephesians 2:8

Scriptures build faith. Proverbs says, "As a man thinketh in his Heart, So is he". The more that a Believer's heart is filled with God's word the better your foundation for life. The Holy Spirit is inside you to reveal the gifts GOD has for you but the Holy Spirit will not do your prayers, worship, conversation with God, speak the word, or read your bible.

Do you feel like God does not hear your prayers?

One of the largest problems in the Body of Christ is setting a personal goal and then asking GOD to bless your goal. When GOD says if you will set a goal based on a word from the Bible or a word from the Holy Spirit your goal and the power to attain the goal is already blessed.

When Peter looked at Jesus walking on the water and said "If it be you bid me come". And Jesus said "Come", there was enough

The Atomic Power of Love, 93

power in that word from GOD for Peter to walk on the water in the midst of a great storm in Peters life. Matthew 14:28

The Apostle Paul says "Let us fear lest we lest we live and die without reaching what God promised us." Hebrews 4:1

Most Christians haven't found out what GOD has for Believers because they accepted the fear of failure instead of fearing living without what GOD has for Believers. Listen to the following scriptures giving Believers a glimpse into the power in the Spiritual world.

Example of power Believers have not even imagined; he (Jesus) was hungry: And seeing a fig tree afar off having leaves, he came, if haply he might find anything thereon: and when he came to it, he found nothing but leaves; for the time of figs was not yet.

And **Jesus answered and said unto it,** NO MAN EAT FRUIT OF THEE HEREAFTER FOREVER. And his disciples heard it. Mark 11:13-14

Notice: A plant spoke to Jesus and **Jesus answered the Fig tree and then spoke to it,** the same authority in Jesus is inside Believers, authority over everything on the earth. You may be saying okay but that was Jesus but the scriptures indicate that same power is inside Believers.

Another example; And Peter, fastening his eyes upon him with John, said, **Look on us.** And he gave heed unto them, expecting to receive something of them. Then Peter said, **Silver and gold have I none; but such as I have give I thee: In the name of Jesus Christ of Nazareth rise up and walk.** And he took him by the right hand, and lifted him up: and immediately his feet and ankle bones received strength. And he leaping up stood, and walked, and entered with them into the temple, walking, and leaping, and praising God. Acts 3:4-8

Notice; Peter spoke in the name and authority he had through Jesus Christ to speak to this man's affliction and said "rise and walk".

Another example; Now the serpent was more crafty than any other beast of the field that the LORD God had made. He said to the woman, "Did God actually say, 'You shall not eat of any tree in the garden'?" And the woman said to the serpent, "We may eat of the fruit of the trees in the garden, Genesis 3:1-2

Notice; Eve is having a conversation with a snake. Believers do not even consider the idea that GOD commissioned Mankind to be fruitful and subdue the earth. GOD had given mankind power over everything under the earth on the earth and in the air.

If you can't picture in your mind the authority of Believers you will not be able to execute more than what you believe. Your mind pictures what it experiences whether physically or in the Spirit, You know whether you are hot or cold, happy or sad, sleepy or rested but what force do you credit for who and whose you are? You can see, hear, and feel, the world and its complexity; the seed bearing plants and trees and all their fruit; the heavens and their majesty; the seasons, the rainbows, the stars at night and the sun at noonday? When you picture the Earth from sea to shining sea, **does your mental picture include GOD or just trip advisor?**

Remember, Remember, Remember.

Nothing lives or moves without GOD. Everything you touch has billions of atoms moving at incredible speed inside each element controlled by GOD. The chair you sit in is moving at atomic speed while you are sitting in it. God created and is controlling the unseen forces that make this world operate for your enjoyment. **Believers must fill our minds with pictures that connect us to the greatness of our GOD.**

Listen to the words from "O what a beautiful morning"; **written by Rogers and Hammerstein but inspired by GOD.**

> There's a bright, golden haze on the meadow
> There's a bright, golden haze on the meadow.
> The corn is as high as an elephant's eye
> And it looks like it's climbing clear up to the sky.
>
> Oh, what a beautiful Mornin'
> Oh, what a beautiful day.
> I've got a beautiful feelin'
> Everything's goin' my way.
>
> All the cattle are standin' like statues
> All the cattle are standin' like statues
> They don't turn their heads as they see me ride by
> But a little brown mav'rick is winkin' her eye

Oh, what a beautiful Mornin'
Oh, what a beautiful day.
I've got a beautiful feelin'
Everything's goin' my way.

All the sounds of the earth are like music
All the sounds of the earth are like music
The breeze is so busy it don't miss a tree
An' a ol' weepin' willer is laughin' at me

Oh, what a beautiful Mornin'
Oh, what a beautiful day.
I've got a beautiful feelin'
Everything's goin' my way.
Oh, what a beautiful day!

You can picture the Creator GOD in this song from beginning to end. As the song says "Oh what a beautiful day" Everything GOD made is beautiful in its truth and fulfillment and GOD made it for you. Contemplate the intricate details GOD put in place to cause this day to unfold. Einstein is credited with saying something similar to "You would have to be an idiot to look at this creation and not believe there is a creator."

You Look Marvelous

Are you always judging yourself by what you see in the mirror? Do you think that God is looking at you from inside the mirror? **GOD is inside you and when you look in the mirror God sees a reflection of his own image.** Can you comprehend that the Eternal new creation life in your body is perfect, sinless, and a beautiful creation of Almighty GOD. The only reflection that matters is that "picture of truth" found in the Bible describing you as being made in the Image of GOD.

The new creation picture is confusing because your body is not a new creation, you are as fat as you were ten minutes ago, your address has not changed, and your car did not become new. The difference is your body is no longer the primary "you", your body is the Carrier for your new Spirit. God is not dealing with Believers according to your performance but

The Atomic Power of Love, 96

instead **GOD is looking at your determination to rest in God's ability to be your sufficiency.** Galatians 4:6, 1 John 4:17, 1 Corinthians 13:10, Romans 8:9, Ephesians 4:24 The judgment for Believers is to determine your reward in Heaven and it is the good works done with the interconnection of your Spirit and your renewed mind. Remember, judgment for Believers is not about sin because that judgment was paid by Jesus Christ, 2,000 years ago, and the payment accepted when you became a Believer. The "bema seat" judgement for Believers is for rewards for Believers, there is no sin in the account of Believers.

A Believer, who has a word or confidence in one of God's promises, can act with the power of Almighty GOD in concert to accomplish the word or promise of GOD. Our existence on earth started with us being slaves to a "nature of sin", now our existence on earth is to be dedicated to "Jesus Christ", who is evidenced in the world through love. Our daily struggle is with controlling every motivation for action or word that directs Believers toward or away from the acting in Love. The entire natural world has changed for the Believer, we are no longer in a fight with flesh and blood, our struggles are against spiritual forces fighting for your mind and emotions. Your ability to reign in life is to draw from God's Words in your heart the power to know what is GOOD and do it.

Constantly remind yourself

As Believers, our Spirits are alive; we have a new Father, Brother, and Friend and Believers can start our prayers "Our Father". In addition, the curse has been reversed, because of Adam breaking covenant with GOD. Believers can see the effects of the curse; we can see the deterioration in our bodies and our earthly world. The Television news gives us a daily account of evil and the corruption of the world, but Believers have been redeemed from the curse, when living in the Spirit.

In contrast, in our new Spiritual life there is no death, no time, and **our future is secure.** Our new Spirit life is outside time (Eternal) but our bodies are subject to time and deterioration. The new battle for Believers is for our thought life which governs the issues of life in our heart. The Believer's interconnection between our Spirit and a Believer's renewed mind allows the knowledge through Jesus Christ to reign over any and all issues of life. Do not let religion keep you from believing in unimaginable gifts from GOD to be used in your life. If you believe that GOD will raise your dead body from the grave and make you a new body and take you to Heaven in the Rapture of the Saints, don't allow someone who does not believe in the manifestation of GODs power, tell you about miracles having passed away. **The people who don't believe, receive what they do believe.** The Believer who does believe that there is power to affect the seen world with the power of your Spirit and GOD's Spirit teaming up to; heal the sick, raise the dead, cast out demons, preach the Gospel to the poor, reign in life and more, as the word of God declares, will have what they believe.

The Sermon on the Mount
Is not instructions for Salvation!

Jesus in the greatest sermon ever given was not setting up a new set of requirements to add to the sin consciousness and condemnation from the Torah but was acting as our High Priest and blessing His people. **Jesus has not yet been sacrificed and resurrected to set forth the way to Salvation,** so this sermon is a presentation of Christian discipleship which can be wrought in the soul of an individual only by the power of God when loving GOD. This poetic message does not tell one 'how to be saved'; it tells one "what it is like to repent and have a relationship with GOD". It explains the quality of the life, offered by the saving grace of God. Its basic truths are reiterated everywhere throughout the New Testament epistles. In the Matthew 5 Sermon, The Lord speaks in parables; principles and patterns.

> **For example:** Ye are the light of the world. A city that is set on a hill cannot be hid. Neither do men light a candle, and put it under a bushel, but on a candlestick; nor does it give light unto all that are in the house.

All of the Bible is useful to believers to deal with the affairs of life in principles and patterns the Lord has given believers by His word which is by faith and a gift of Grace.

Principles (Explain what makes things work or why things happen) and
> Patterns (Model, design, or blueprints show the way things happen)

result in Keys
to unlock mysteries
and reveal the Truth.

**GOD gave Moses the Law
which set up the way to live in Israel
Now GOD has eliminated
the law and effects of sin, for the Believer.
Now we are living in the Love of GOD.**

In whom we have redemption through his blood, even the forgiveness of sins: Who is the image of the invisible God, the firstborn of every creature: For by him were all things created, that are in heaven, and that are in earth, visible and invisible, whether they be thrones, or dominions, or principalities, or powers: all things were created by him, and for him: And he is before all things, and by him all things consist. And he is the head of the body, the church: who is the beginning, the firstborn from the dead; that in all things he might have the preeminence. Colossians 1:14-19

Today there is more knowledge of GOD and the Bible than any time in history. The new knowledge Believers have harvested, from the Word of God has exposed that the foundation of our religion is an incomplete teaching of our Salvation and the Kingdom of GOD.

For Example, the recent changes in knowledge;
The lack of teaching about the Holy Spirit abiding in Believers available on earth 24/7, in contrast to asking GOD to come down from Heaven to rescue Believers.
The concept of the rapture is only 140 years old.
Israel became a nation in its homeland nearly 2000 years after being dispersed by the Romans in 70 AD. Answering many prophesies.
Bibles are available to everyone.

The Atomic Power of Love, 99

The knowledge of Grace has begun to change the Sin Conscious, Performance based teaching.

The Sabbath day has been expanded to a Sabbath every day because GOD is in you making rest available daily.

Presently, the enemy has had Mankind for 6 days a week and we have given ourselves to GOD one day a week and that allotment of time is all wrong.

For example: Before Jesus went to the cross, When Jesus was speaking to the rich young ruler who had asked about receiving Eternal life, Jesus said, " Do the commandments….sell what you have and follow me". After the cross, the jailer in Acts asked Paul and Silas what must I do to be saved and Paul said, "Believe in the Lord Jesus and you will be saved, you and your house." The new battleground is in a Believer's mind.

What is meant by Paul's words in Ephesians 6:12

> For we **wrestle not against flesh and blood,** but against principalities, against powers, against the rulers of the darkness of this world, against **spiritual wickedness in high places.** Ephesians 6:12.

Notice the question is not what do I do about my food, clothing, and shelter but How do I fight against Spiritual world problems? Until Believers rule over their Spiritual World, Believers cannot rule over their physical world.

You must Believe: To act on trust in GOD   Romans 12:2

> GOD created the world with His words and owns everything.
>> When a believer gives he does not lose anything because he does not own anything, he is only a steward giving of the Lords substance.
>
> Jesus died for your sin and offers right standing with GOD
>> GOD made your New Spirit righteous and perfect.
>> Your identity is not your actions it is what GOD made you,
>
> GOD wants a relationship with you
> GOD wants to supply your daily needs
> GOD has a purpose for your life.

If supplying your needs is easy for you then you probably have not found God's purpose for your life.

**Faith will only appropriate
what GOD has already provided
in the atonement.
Faith is our positive response and activates what God
has already provided.
Believers must labor to rest (faith)
in GOD's sufficiency**

Chapter 6

You are GOD's Beloved (Phil 2:12)
GOD did not give you the Grace for Salvation
To punish you with lack, poverty, and bad health.

Joseph, most favored son of Jacob, was thrown in a pit and prospered, was sold into slavery and prospered, was thrown into prison and prospered. **Your daily situation does not determine your prosperity, but your relationship with GOD determines your total well-being. Listen to these five scriptures about a relationship with GOD.**

> **Psalm 23:5** Thou preparest a table before me in the presence of mine enemies: thou anointest my head with oil; my cup runneth over. Surely goodness and mercy shall follow me all the days of my life: and I will dwell in the house of the LORD forever.
>
> **Romans 8:28** Furthermore, we know that **God causes everything to work together for the good of those who love God and are called in accordance with his purpose;** because those whom he knew in advance, he also determined in advance would be conformed to the pattern of his Son, so that he might be the firstborn among many brothers; **and those whom he thus determined in advance, he also called; and those whom he called, he also caused to be considered righteous; and those whom he caused to be considered righteous he also glorified!** What, then, are we to say to these things? **If God is for us, who can be against us?** He who did not spare even his own Son, but gave him up on behalf of us all — is it possible that, **having given us his Son, he would not give us everything else too?** So who will bring a charge against God's chosen people? Certainly not God — he is the one who causes them to be considered righteous! Who punishes them? Certainly not the Messiah Jesus, who died and — more than that — has been raised, is at the right hand of God and is actually pleading on our behalf!

Who will **separate us from the love of the Messiah?**
Shall Trouble?
Hardship?
Persecution?
Hunger?
Poverty?
Danger?
War?....
"No, in all these things we are super conquerors,
through the one who has loved us.
For I am convinced
that neither death nor life,
neither angels nor other heavenly rulers,
neither what exists nor what is coming,
neither powers above nor powers below,
nor any other created thing will be able
to separate us from **the love of God**
which comes to us through the Messiah, Jesus Christ.

Psalms 32:1 [By David.] How blessed are those **whose offense is forgiven,** those whose sin is covered! How blessed those **to whom GOD imputes no guilt,** in whose spirit is no deceit!
Romans 4:6 In the same way, the blessing which David pronounces is on those **whom God credits with righteousness** apart from legalistic observances: **"Blessed are those whose transgressions are forgiven, whose sins are covered over; Blessed is the man whose sin GOD will not reckon against his account."**
For the promise to Abraham and his seed that he would inherit the world did not come through legalism but **through the righteousness that trust produces.** For if the heirs are produced by legalism, then trust is pointless and the promise worthless. For what law brings is punishment. But where there is no law, there is also no violation. The reason the promise is based on trusting is so that it may come as God's free gift, a promise that can be relied on by all the seed, not only those who live within the framework of

the Torah, but also those with the kind of trust Abraham had—Abraham, our father, for all of us. Romans 4:13-16

A Believer's inheritance from Jesus Christ

Salvation Benefit- No Condemnation
Salvation Benefit-GOD condemned sin in the flesh.

Romans 8:1 **There is therefore now no condemnation to them which are in Christ Jesus,** who walk not after the flesh, but after the Spirit. For the law of the Spirit of life in Christ Jesus hath made me free from the law of sin and death. For what the law could not do, in that it was weak through the flesh, God sending his own Son in the likeness of sinful flesh, and for sin, **condemned sin in the flesh:** That the righteousness of the law might be fulfilled in us, who walk not after the flesh, but after the Spirit.

Salvation Benefit- Redeemed from the Curse of the Torah (law)
Salvation Benefit- Gentiles also received the Promise of Abraham.

Galatians 3:9 So then, those who rely on trusting and being faithful are blessed along with Abraham, who trusted and was faithful. For everyone who depends on legalistic observance of Torah commands lives under a curse, since it is written, "Cursed is everyone who does not keep on doing everything written in the Scroll of the Torah." Now it is evident that no one comes to be declared righteous by God through legalism, since "The person who is righteous will attain life by trusting and being faithful." Furthermore, legalism is not based on trusting and being faithful, but on [a misuse of] the text that says, "Anyone who does these things will attain life through them." **The Messiah redeemed us from the curse pronounced in the Torah by becoming cursed on our behalf; for the Old Testament says, "Everyone who hangs from a stake comes under a curse."** Jesus, the Messiah did this so that in union with him the Gentiles might receive the blessing announced to Abraham, so that through trusting and being faithful, we might receive what was promised, namely, the Spirit.

Scriptures can drive out doubt in your heart, to give your belief system room for the prompting of the Holy Spirit to believe, all that is written, in the Bible concerning the Lord Jesus Christ. There is a peace offered from a relationship with GOD Almighty and studying His Word and meditating in His love keeps believers in the midst of the Peace of GOD.

You believe in the bread recipe of water, flour, and yeast to be mixed together and produce bread, but did you know that none of the individual parts taste good and they don't look good to eat but when the molecules and enzymes God made, go to work, the ingredients react to each ingredient to make wonderful bread. Jesus is the Bread of Life and he is giving us the recipe for the fully developed abundant life. Believe, gain knowledge, meditate and you will receive the abundant life, it is a gift you just have to know what it entails.

Salvation Benefit-The Holy Spirit is in you to convict you of Jesus righteousness in you. John 16:5-10,

The Holy Spirit is not here to convict the Christians of their Sin because He has already accomplished that before you became a Believer. He is here to convict you of **"the righteousness"** you received from the overpayment of your sins ; past, present, and future by the gift of Jesus Christ. When you see in your Spirit the love and sacrifice made just for you, that intimacy with GOD, The Holy Spirit, and Savior and belief will produce your daily "Living Bread". And that intimacy with the Holy Spirit will keep your belief in the gift of Righteousness before your Spiritual eyes and you will "live right" because you believe right.

Contemplate the PURPOSE of the gift of the Holy Spirit as you read John 16

> I have yet many things to say unto you, but ye cannot bear them now. Howbeit when he, the Spirit of truth, is come, he will guide you into all truth: for he shall not speak of himself; but whatsoever he shall hear, that shall he speak: and he will shew you things to come. He shall glorify me: for he shall receive of mine, **and shall shew it unto you.** John 16:15 All things that the Father hath are mine: therefore said I, **that he shall take of mine, and shall shew it unto you.**

Salvation Benefit-The Holy spirit will show you the things of GOD and the things to come

Now we must learn to hear the Holy Spirit, We must open up communication with the Holy Spirit. You read and can understand the Job of the Holy Spirit is to show you all things of Truth, GOD, and things to come, but it will not benefit you if you are not listening in your heart to the Holy Spirit and not absorbing God's word so that you can understand the TRUTH. **For example** develop a constant conversation with God and expect answers, and be still to hear and feel the leading of the Spirit.

For example: Start every day
    with a conversation with God
        asking for direction,
            a prayer, praise, and thanksgiving
                giving a blessing on your house,
            spouse, children, and their families,
And asking the holy Spirit to reveal to you one of the gifts GOD has for you.

**These are the Facts,
Just the Facts, and
Nothing but the Facts.
GOD loves you.**

Chapter 7

Miracles are not miraculous!
If you have
A Word from GOD

Believers have been given a word from GOD
The fact that water became wine, or
    5,000 people were fed from five small loaves and two fish, or
        four people were raised from the dead or
            after fishing all night without a catch throwing the
            net on the other side of the boat brought in a net
            breaking load of fish,

These and many more miracles are compassion at work in Jesus. The miraculous aspects of the Spiritual world are evident when we think about a Believer's relationship with GOD. Can you speak about any of the following questions without saying miracle? What is the answer to **"How can we abide in GOD and GOD abide in Believers? Or How can Believers be new creations? How can our sins be forgiven and we are now eternal? Scripture announces** "We are seated together with Jesus Christ in Heavenly places", and yet, do you experience any reality in being seated with Jesus Christ in the Heavenlies? If Believers don't believe "Who they are in Jesus?" then Believers will not believe they are seated with Jesus in Heavenly places.

If Believers are not talking to Jesus, sharing with the Holy Spirit, worshipping Almighty GOD, looking for GOD's direction seven days a week, then you are depending on your own ability and you are missing the love GOD wants to give you. To experience what GOD has for Believers we must love GOD and receive love from GOD and let GOD supply all the daily needs of life. That is what "Trusting in GOD" is all about.

You are a "made man"
And you know the real GODfather.

The Atomic Power of Love, 107

The only way believers can be seated with Christ in Heaven and be alive on Earth is to understand and embrace the omnipresent realm of "being" that is in common with the "New Creation" in Mankind. **I am not saying believers are omnipresent in the entire world,** but I am saying there is a part of GOD's omnipresence that believers share, when we abide in GOD and HE abides in Believers. Jesus Christ made your "New Creation life" perfect. Listen to this scripture about our flesh and our heavenly body.

> For we know that if our earthly house of this tabernacle were dissolved, we **have a building of God, an house not made with hands, eternal in the heavens.** For in this we groan, earnestly **desiring to be clothed upon with our house which is from heaven (our resurrected body):** 2nd Corinthians 5:1

To complicate our need to find ourselves and the worlds we live inside, listen to this scripture from 1st John 4:15.

> Whosoever shall confess that Jesus is the Son of God, **God dwelleth in him,** and **he in God.** And we have known and believed the love that God hath to us. **God is love;** and **he that dwelleth in love dwelleth in God, and God in him.** Herein is our love made perfect, that we may have boldness in the Day of Judgment: because **as he (Jesus) is, so are we (Believers) in this world.**

When we consider that **as Jesus "is" in this world, so are Believers;** "How is Jesus in the Physical and Spiritual world?" <u>**The answer is Jesus is the invisible force that is revealed in the love in Believers and their actions of goodness.**</u>

Believers have discovered part of the unseen structures of The Atomic world and the Gene sequencing (DNA) in our physical world and now we are discovering the unseen power of the Spirit World. Love (the perfectness of Goodness), which is the opposite of evil, is the building block of the Spiritual Kingdom. Do not allow this unseen force to frighten you but instead realize that the "Creator of all" created you and the Spiritual World and greater is He that is in you than he that is in the world. Listen to the Apostle Paul tell Believers **who you are in Jesus.**

> So who will bring a charge against God's chosen people? Certainly not God — he is the one who causes them to be considered righteous! Who punishes them? Certainly not the Messiah Jesus

Christ, who died and — more than that — has been raised, is at the right hand of God and is actually pleading on our behalf! **Who will separate us from the love of the Messiah Jesus Christ?** Trouble? Hardship? Persecution? Hunger? Poverty? Danger? War? …. No, in all these things **we are superconquerors,** through the one who has loved us.

For I am convinced that neither death nor life, neither angels nor **other heavenly rulers,** neither what exists nor what is coming, neither powers above nor powers below, nor **any other created thing** will be able to **separate us from the love of God** which comes to us through the Messiah Jesus Christ. Romans 8:33-39

Believers can reign from their position in the Kingdom and in the Heart of Almighty GOD, Jesus Christ, and the Holy Spirit. The love of the Kingdom for Believers is the power that created the world, motivated Jesus to die for the sin of Mankind and to create Believers in the image of GOD.

If God said it;
Believers must believe it, and imagine it.

The "Finished works of Jesus Christ" are voice activated. The Holy Spirit and a Believer's Spirit are inside Believers and use the voice and actions of the body to affect the seen world with the unseen power of the Spirit. As we study and explore all the Lord's gifts of Grace, we will begin to understand that GOD created the worlds and GOD powers everything in the worlds. All the elements that Mankind uses for business and pleasure perform functions that GOD designed for the pleasure of his children. For example: water plus heat is used to clean, cook, sterilize, humidify, dissolve, and many more uses. Mankind did not make any of the element characteristics for water or fire. Believers exist in several dimensions and the innate workings of the materials, forces, and requirements in each dimension are controlled by Jesus Christ.

Physical or atomic world created a habitat for Mankind.

This is the atomic, molecular, and elemental world of the Cosmos, the heavens and atmosphere, the earth and its moon, from the atoms and molecules to the elements, rocks and soil, mountains and oceans, plant life and animals.

> The laws that operate; atoms, molecules, seeds, and elements, et cetera are preprogrammed in their make-up supplied by GOD. The results of the preprogrammed nature of our natural world are e v i d e n t b u t t h e programing can't be seen.

For example: when you mix water, wheat flower, and yeast and let the dough sit and then bake, the programming in those ingredients will make bread. This is a gift from GOD; mankind had nothing to do with programming those ingredients. Understanding the building blocks of the Spiritual World and their preprogrammed characteristics will allow Believers to manifest Spiritual end products.

> **Spiritual world where the inhabitants are eternal.** Spirits do not have biological needs <u>unless the Spirit is residing in a body.</u> The Spiritual world has no atmospheric boundaries and time is not a factor. In the Spiritual world, it is not actions that allow entrance, but by the act of choosing whom you serve that determines whose you are. The Kingdom of GOD is a family place.

> **The Laws operating in the Spiritual world** are
> "Love your GOD with everything and your neighbor as yourself.
> There are no curses operating in this world for Believers.
> There are no unsaved humans in this world.
> Acts of kindness, by Believers, and love in the natural world accumulate to the account of the doer in the Spiritual world.
> Persecutions for being a Believer in the Natural world accumulate to the account of the doer in the Spiritual world.
> Martyrdom for your belief in Jesus Christ is celebrated and added to the account of the doer in the Spiritual world.

Believers did absolutely nothing without using the gifts of GOD; we use our minds to design a project that will be built out of products GOD made with the properties that GOD gave the materials to react. Again, think about the bread example, believers mix water and flour and a leavener together and heat it up and we think we made the bread, but GOD made all three items and their properties and gave us the idea to put them together. When we see what happened to the dough and smell and taste the wonderful bread, it should be evident to us that God made the bread. The beauty of a loaf of bread to the eye, nose, and to the taste must develop pictures in our minds that keep us in awe of the God of Creation, who has done everything to provide for our bodies, reconciliation with Him, and relationship for our internal Spirit. Believers must strip out our man-made ability and accomplishment from the "New Creation Life" given to believers and live in "Thanksgiving" for what GOD has given Believers.

> **Ephesians 5:17** Wherefore be ye not unwise, **but understanding what the will of the Lord is.** And be not drunk with wine, wherein is excess; but be filled with the Spirit; Speaking to ourselves in psalms and hymns and spiritual songs, singing and making melody in your heart to the Lord; **Giving thanks always for all things unto God and the Father in the name of our Lord Jesus Christ;**

Believers must behold our God and Savior.

When we bless our food and give the credit and praise to GOD for the food we eat, the clothes we wear, the place we sleep, and the love we feel; we are building a picture of GOD as our provider. When you think about the making of bread in the last example, you can see how lame it is for believers to think that we made the bread ourselves. **We put the ingredients in a pan, God made it be bread.** GOD loves us with a love that will grow in every picture we develop in our mind of what GOD has made for Believers.

The story is told, that a Pastor from the Park Cities went to a poor country on a mission trip and at the end of the trip was talking to the Pastor from the local church from which he had worked, and he asked if he could pray for the prosperity of his church. The pastor said it would be a blessing to have his prayers and that he would like to pray for the Park Cities church. The Pastor from the poor church, started thanking GOD for the miraculous provision of food for every meal and shelter every day in answer to the daily prayers of each parishioner and entreated GOD to allow the Park

Cities Church to experience the glory from receiving miraculous answer to prayer every day, for every morsel of food article of clothing, and place to lay their head. The Park Cities Pastor then realized that the richest Church might not be his Church.

Our perception of "normal" as American Christians is skewed from the prosperity of our country and we must realize that GOD is moved by the depth of a Believer's relationship with GOD and not by the richness of the surroundings of the Believers. The Believers of the Church in the Southern Hemisphere had to look to GOD every day for everything, and knew or beheld God as their provider. In America knowing GOD as our provider is more difficult because of the ease of provision of a Believer's basic needs. Not beholding GOD as our provider makes needing GOD as our Healer or Protector or Total Wellbeing nearly impossible because our relationship with GOD is lacking. The problem for America is that instead of reaching out to GOD for our total wellbeing mankind has abandoned prayer and depended on the government for provision.

You don't own what you think you own, but you have inherited a Kingdom and its throne.

Whatever assets Believers think we own were not owned by the seller, who sold them to us. GOD did not sell or give his creation to any person to own. Our stay on Earth is a time given to each person for which there is going to be an accounting of how Mankind used GOD's creation.

Do not settle for the man-made prosperity, Believers may be able to provide for your daily needs, that are here today and eaten before tomorrow, but instead pray for and receive the God created total well-being available to those who give of their substance to others and receive abundance from GOD.

> Chronicles 29:11 Thine O Lord is the greatness, the power, the glory, the victory and the majesty; for everything in heaven and on earth is yours. The kingdom is yours, O Lord; and you are exalted as head over all. Riches and honor come from you, you rule everything, in your hand is power and strength, you have the capacity to make great and to give strength to all. Now, therefore, our God, we thank you and praise your glorious name. "But who

The Atomic Power of Love, 112

am I, and what is my people, that we should be able to give so willingly in this way? For all things come from you, **so that we have given you what is already yours.**
Even, when we give to GOD in substance, time, money, or praise, et cetera; we are only giving back, what GOD has given to Believers. Anything Believers do, touch, give, grow, or make is accomplished with ingredients from the Lord. The prayer indicates that when we give things to the Lord, that are already His, that act of Honor and love, we get blessed **because we have beheld our Father GOD.** It does not make sense to the material world, but it does to our Father.

Can you skip over working to provide your daily needs to embrace the giver of Eternal life and the gifts He has for you? **For example: Think about GOD's provision during the life of Jesus;** Jesus supported a large entourage, paid taxes, had a treasurer, gave to the poor, made wine, wore expensive clothes, did not take up offerings, and much more. The first action of Jesus was to seek His Father and His righteousness and all of the issues of provision were added by His Father GOD. Believers have been given gifts for which we will give an accounting.

> And from Jesus Christ, who is the faithful witness, and the first begotten of the dead, and the prince of the kings of the earth. Unto him that loved us, and washed us from our sins in his own blood, And hath made us kings and priests unto God and his Father; to him be glory and dominion for ever and ever. Amen. Revelation 1:5-6

Does this scripture make you question the path you are on? The wording is incontrovertible, it is for Believers and it is for today. What shall we do with power of a King and the closeness to GOD of a Priest?

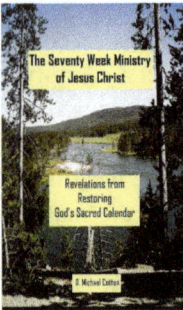

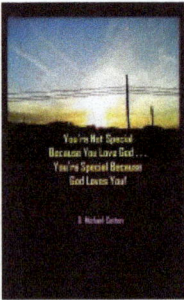

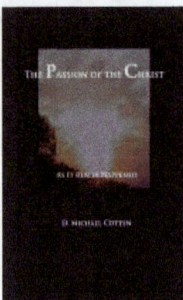

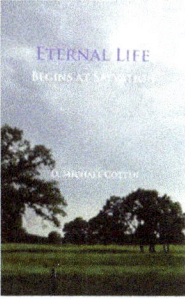

Eternal Life Begins at Salvation
by Michael Cotten
ISBN# 978-1-936497-25-6
101 pages, $14.99

Contact the Author at
dmichaelcotten@att.net

Searchlight Press
Who are you looking for?
Publishers of thoughtful Christian books since 1994.
PO Box 554
Henderson, TX 75652-0554
888.896.6081
info@Searchlight-Press.com
www.Searchlight-Press.com

www.ingramcontent.com/pod-product-compliance
Lightning Source LLC
LaVergne TN
LVHW022012080426
835513LV00009B/684